# THE Accidental Veterinarian

## TALES FROM A PET PRACTICE

# Philipp Schott DVM

Published by ECW Press
665 Gerrard Street East
Toronto, Ontario, Canada M4M 1Y2
416-694-3348 / info@ecwpress.com

To the best of his abilities, the author has related
experiences, places, people, and organizations
from his memories of them. In order to protect the
privacy of others, he has, in some instances, changed
the names of certain people and details of events
and places.

Cover design: David A. Gee
Interior Illustrations: Brian Gable

LIBRARY AND ARCHIVES CANADA
CATALOGUING IN PUBLICATION

Schott, Philipp, author
        The accidental veterinarian : tales
from a pet practice / Philipp Schott.

Issued also in print and electronic formats.
ISBN 978-1-77041-480-8 (softcover)
ISBN 978-1-77305-342-4 (PDF)
ISBN 978-1-77305-341-7 (ePUB)

1. Veterinary medicine—Anecdotes. 2.
Pets—Anecdotes. 3. Veterinary medicine—
Miscellanea. 4. Pets—Miscellanea. 5.
Veterinarians—Manitoba—Biography.
I. Title.

SF745.S32 2019            636.089
C2018-905304-6        C2018-905305-4

This book is not intended to be a substitute
for professional veterinary advice,
diagnosis, or treatment. Always consult
your veterinarian with any questions you
may have regarding the medical condition
of your pet.

The publication of *The Accidental Veterinarian* has been generously supported by the Canada
Council for the Arts which last year invested $153 million to bring the arts to Canadians throughout
the country and is funded in part by the Government of Canada. *Nous remercions le Conseil des
arts du Canada de son soutien. L'an dernier, le Conseil a investi 153 millions de dollars pour mettre
de l'art dans la vie des Canadiennes et des Canadiens de tout le pays. Ce livre est financé en partie
par le gouvernement du Canada.* We acknowledge the support of the Ontario Arts Council (OAC),
an agency of the Government of Ontario, which last year funded 1,737 individual artists and 1,095
organizations in 223 communities across Ontario for a total of $52.1 million. We also acknowledge
the contribution of the Government of Ontario through the Ontario Book Publishing Tax Credit, and
through Ontario Creates for the marketing of this book.

PRINTED AND BOUND IN CANADA            PRINTING: MARQUIS  5  4  3  2

*For Lorraine, who began this adventure with me
and has been there every step of the way
and will be for every step to come.*

"When all t'world goes one road, I go t'other."

— JAMES HERRIOT,
*All Creatures Great and Small*

# Contents

# PREFACE

I graduated from the Western College of Veterinary Medicine in Saskatoon in 1990. I had been writing a little for years, but after finishing school I suddenly found that I had a lot more free time, so I began to write more regularly. For 25 years, veterinary medicine and writing ran like twinned parallel streams, each just out of sight of the other. I wrote about travel, and I wrote about whisky. I wrote a children's chapter book, and I wrote short stories. But it never occurred to me to write about my job. In retrospect, I think I feared the intermingling of work with my private life, as veterinary medicine can become a monster that eats your life, if you allow it to do so. I had seen that happen too often. But over time, I noticed more and more that people wanted me to tell my vet stories, not my travel stories (and certainly not my whisky stories).

Veterinary medicine is a story machine. People are often at their most human around animals. I've had hardened-looking men confess that they cried more when their dog died than when their father died, and I've had lonely elderly women say that they have laughed more with their kitten than they have about anything else in their lives for a very long time. And the animals themselves, the unwitting central players in these dramas and comedies, are of course endlessly fascinating, endlessly charming, endlessly appealing. The writer in me could not ignore this reality anymore, so two years ago I started a veterinary blog, from which many of the following stories and essays are drawn. And to my delight, the monster has not eaten my life. In my case, it instead turned out to be a complicated but gentle beast, and it has enriched my life, as my life has always enriched my work.

# PART I

# THE MAKING OF A VETERINARIAN

## BOBO THE CHRISTMAS GERBIL

Like most children and almost every veterinarian, I was fascinated with animals from a very young age. And like most children, my fascination spawned a relentless campaign to obtain a pet. My parents were, however, not "pet people." Far from it. My parents didn't have pets growing up (it was war-torn Germany after all — there were many other priorities, like survival), and none of the people they knew once we immigrated to Saskatoon had pets. It simply wasn't part of their world. They didn't view pet ownership as a bad thing, necessarily, but it was something "other people" did, like line dancing or cross-dressing. A dog was so clearly out of the question that I never actually dared to ask, and I understood that the suggestion of a cat would be received no differently than a suggestion of a warthog or a rhesus monkey. So I set my sights lower and began the work of building up the Mongolian gerbil as the ideal pet in my parents' minds.

This prolonged effort had no discernible effect whatsoever until Christmas of 1977, when a large, rectangular object covered by a decidedly non-festive grey tablecloth appeared under the tree. I had more or less given up on the gerbil campaign by that point. I was actually afraid that the large rectangular object would be a gigantic Meccano set as part of my father's own campaign to get me interested in something "practical." But no — to my astonishment, the object revealed itself to be a cage. A large cage, hand-built by my father out of heavy gauge one-inch galvanized steel mesh. This cage was solid. It appeared to be designed to help its occupant withstand earthquakes, tornadoes, mortar attacks and significant civil unrest.

But there was no occupant.

"Oh wow! Thank you, thank you! It's a . . . It's a . . . It's an empty cage."

My parents peered closely at the cage and then looked at each other. There had been a gerbil in there just half an hour ago. Now there was no gerbil. My father, the physicist, expressed astonishment and disbelief that a gerbil could pop through one-inch mesh. But pop through it evidently had, like a button through a buttonhole. The remaining gift openings and assorted Christmas rituals were abandoned, and the hunt was on. Two bewildered adults and two manic children scoured the house until eventually the gerbil was found, pooping silently in a corner under a cabinet.

Incidentally, as an aside for the uninitiated, a Mongolian gerbil is a small desert rodent (I first wrote "dessert rodent," and it slipped by the spellchecker as well) with tan-coloured fur and a long tail ending in a fuzzy tuft, a bit like a lion's tail. They bite a lot less than hamsters, and they stink a lot less than mice.

As soon as the gerbil was captured, my father set to work covering the cage with fly screen. This was effective for a day or two, but then the gerbil chewed through the fly screen. It was patched and patched again, but the gerbil was nothing if not relentless. What eventually put a stop to his repeated escapes were sunflower seeds. Or, more precisely, the morbid obesity caused by the continuous intake of high-fat sunflower seeds. He soon became unable to squeeze his bulk through that mesh anymore. So he stayed in the cage, exchanging his freedom for tasty snacks. A trade-off familiar to Doritos addicts everywhere.

Over time, the gerbil and I became close. Or, more accurately, I should say that I became close to him; for his part, I think it's safe to say that the gerbil was largely indifferent to me — or really anything other than his sunflower seeds. I originally named him "Berbil," but this morphed into "Berbo" and then "Bobo," which is ultimately the version that stuck.

Eventually Bobo died and was not replaced. The cage ended up in the basement with the suitcases and old coffee makers and was forgotten until one bitterly cold January morning when my father found a pocket gopher, an essentially blind burrowing animal that should have been hibernating but was out wandering in disoriented circles on a snowy field. My father dusted off the cage and then, to our collective astonishment, walked out onto the field to scoop up the surprised rodent. Failing to recognize the good deed, it bit him savagely, but my father persisted and brought him inside and placed him carefully in the cage. Ultimately, over the course of the next three or four months, he and the pocket gopher developed a peculiar and, it seems, mutually beneficial relationship. The gopher was released in the spring, and the cage never saw use again. In my mind's eye I picture it in some deep substratum of the Saskatoon landfill, intact, unbroken, still sturdy like the day my father built it.

### THE ACCIDENTAL VETERINARIAN

I did not plan on becoming a veterinarian. In fact, when I was a child, I was only dimly aware of what veterinarians were as we did not have any pets other than the gerbil, for whom professional medical care was honestly never a consideration. For many years I wanted to be a geographer or a historian at a university. Yes, I was a strange child. Then, in high school, my interest in animals and nature, which had always been there at some level, began to grow, and I added zoologist to the list. But veterinarian still wasn't on the radar.

My father was a practical man who had become cynical about academia. He was a physics professor at the University of Saskatchewan, and he believed that academic jobs were going to become increasingly scarce as well as increasingly unappealing due to ballooning university bureaucracy. Consequently, he viewed my interest in pursuing an academic career in zoology, history or geography with growing apprehension. He was fond of the pithy German phrase "Brotlose Kunst," which translates directly as "breadless art" — in other words, a career or job that doesn't put bread on the table. He left the choice up to me but made it clear that he recommended I pursue a profession instead.

I was a freakishly obedient teenager (mostly), so it came to pass that I spent a sunny Saturday morning in March of 1983, the year I graduated from high school, methodically going through the University of Saskatchewan's course calendar. The programs were listed alphabetically. I began eliminating them one by one: Agriculture (boring), Anthropology (Brotlose Kunst), Art (Brotlose Kunst) . . . and so on. As per the proffered advice, I paid particular attention to the professional colleges, but I steadily, inexorably eliminated them all too: Dentistry (ha), Engineering (boring), Medicine (nope — sick people are gross), etc. I was comprehensively alarmed by the time I got to Theology (ha) as I had almost reached the end of the alphabet without finding anything that made sense to me. There was only one program left. I turned the page and saw Veterinary Medicine written there.

Huh. Veterinary Medicine.

I couldn't think of a counterargument. In fact, the more I thought about it, the more appealing the idea became. This was essentially applied zoology! Moreover, I reasoned that I had always liked dogs and cats, although I had never owned one.

In the impulsive way of 17-year-olds, I decided right then that, yes, this was Plan A. It also helped that the father of a girl I had a crush on was a professor at the vet college. But I knew absolutely nothing about the profession. I hadn't even read James Herriot. Incidentally, for the equally uninitiated, James Herriot was the world's most famous and beloved veterinarian in the latter half of the 20th century on the strength of *All Creatures Great and Small*, his bestselling memoirs and the popular BBC TV series based on them. He is perhaps now in danger of being eclipsed by Australia's buff "Bondi Vet," but for people of a certain age, Herriot is the veterinarian against which all others are measured. When I did find out more about veterinary medicine, I began to waver (Herriot had the opposite effect on me than he did on most people) and completed a biology degree first, but my faculty adviser echoed my father's advice — get a profession, go into veterinary medicine like you had planned. And so I did.

The great majority of my colleagues had wanted to be veterinarians for as long as they could remember. In most cases they'd had to move a considerable distance to Saskatoon or Guelph to attend veterinary school. Their plan was clear, and their commitment was strong. In contrast I still marvel at the accidental nature of my entry into the profession, a profession that has not only given me a remarkable career, but through which I met my wife and moved to Winnipeg. What would have happened if the U of S hadn't offered Veterinary Medicine, and the last entry in that course catalogue had been Theology?

Some accidents are happy. This is one of them.

## MOOK

It was a decade after Bobo the gerbil before another pet came into the house (the pocket gopher never being tame enough to be considered a pet). I continued to want a dog, but only in an abstract sort of way as it was simply not going to happen.

Then, while I was starting second-year biology at the University of Saskatchewan, we moved to an acreage about 20 kilometres southwest of the city. It had always been my father's dream to own land and live in the country. Experimental plasma physicist by day, gentleman farmer by night (and weekends and holidays). He began to collect tractors and then outbuildings to house these tractors.

One late autumn day a black-and-white kitten appeared in the tall grass around one of these outbuildings. It was good mousing terrain, I suppose. It was a boy, and it was probably about 10 weeks old. My parents had no idea what to do. I was preoccupied with school and with being a young adult with a car and a social life (such as it was), so I didn't pay too much attention at first. The kitten was extremely friendly. It would run up to you and immediately begin rubbing on your pant leg, purring at an improbable volume for such a small creature. And in the way of cats who hone in on the least cat-friendly person in any given crowd, he took a special liking to my father.

Winter can hit quickly in Saskatchewan, and it can hit hard. After gentle badgering from the rest of us, my father allowed the kitten to come into the detached garage and began to feed him there. He did this himself, saying he was in there all the time anyway. Sure, it was a nuisance, but not much of one. But the kitten was only to be allowed into the garage, nowhere else. Certainly not the house.

Somewhere around this time the kitten acquired a name. We called him Mook (pronounced like "took") because my mother said that was the chirping sound he made when he head-butted your hand: "mook, mook."

I imagine that many of you have already worked out for yourselves where this story is going. You are absolutely right. As winter set in, the garage became quite cold as well. My father said, "OK, the cat can come into the house, but only the basement. Nowhere else." Our basement stairs had a door at the top, so in theory it was relatively simple to keep him down there. Mook would, however, cry pitifully from behind the door. So soon my father said, "Well, during the day Mook can come up on the main floor, but at night he goes down. And he does not go into the bedrooms or my study."

A few weeks later I came home early from a Saturday running errands in town. My mother and brother were still out. When I came in the front door, I heard an odd sound coming from upstairs. It was a shuffling and scraping noise and the sound of my father chuckling, although he was home alone. I went upstairs and saw that the door to my father's study was open. I peeked inside and saw him on his hands and knees, playing with Mook, both of them delighted.

I started veterinary school two years after Mook came into our lives, and he was my constant study companion. He knew exactly where to lie on my desk so that I wouldn't shoo him off. He made some of the abstractions that were being taught seem more real, and he was a source of comfort when I was stressed.

In 1990 I graduated and moved to Winnipeg. Although I called him "my cat," Mook was really more my parents' cat, so there was no question that he would stay. He continued to have adventures on the acreage, including being quite seriously injured when he was either hit by a car or fell out of a tree, we're not sure which. My mother was visiting family in Germany when this happened, so my father nursed him back to health, giving pills, changing bandages and phoning me frequently for updates and advice. My father had never phoned me any other time for any other reason. Something shifted between us when he did this. Two adults talking together, needing each other. My father passed away two years later.

Then in 2002 my daughter, Isabel, was born. Mook was quite old by that point — I suppose 18, when I do the math. During one of the first visits with the baby to Saskatoon, Mook padded into our room and clambered up onto the bed, where I was holding Isabel, trying to settle her to sleep. Mook curled up beside her, purring. I remember so very clearly how grateful I was to him and how strongly I felt the connection from Isabel to my father through this cat. A living link. I couldn't stop myself from crying.

## MAKING THE CALL

I sometimes have difficulty distinguishing which of my distant memories are directly of an event versus which are of seeing photos of that event. For better or worse, however, this is not as much of a problem for the most of the 1980s, when my parents no longer took photos of me or what I was doing, and before I started taking photos myself. My childhood and my adulthood are both lavishly documented, but that in-between period, when I was in high school and university, is largely a gauzy blur from which only a few memories stand out crisply enough that I have been able to hang on to them and cultivate them as way-posts from the era. One of these memories is of me sitting at the tan-coloured rotary dial telephone on the little desk in the front hall of our house in Saskatoon. I was dialling the number of a local veterinary clinic. Or at least I was trying to.

I was in the second year of my pre-veterinary program through the Department of Biology at the University of Saskatchewan. I was still waffling about applying to the Western College of Veterinary Medicine, but I wanted to keep all my options open. Admission to vet school was mostly based on marks, but they did insist that you have at least some experience working or volunteering in a vet clinic, so that you would have some idea of what you were getting yourself into. I had never been inside of one. Not even briefly. Even if I did go to vet school, it was my intent to use it as a springboard for a career in teaching and research in some aspect of veterinary medicine. But clinical exposure was mandatory regardless, so I made a list of the local clinics and their phone numbers, prior-itized by convenience of location. I took this list to the phone and stared at it and stared at the phone. I was terrified. I would begin to dial and then hang up, swear at myself, and then begin to dial again. This was all made worse by the fact that I was extremely self-conscious, so I would only attempt to make the call when none of the rest of my family was home. My mother was almost always home.

It's bizarre to think back on that given how often I have to speak to strangers on the phone now, but at the time the fear absolutely paralyzed me. I doubted that anyone would be interested in having someone with no experience whatsoever hang around their clinic. I imagined these clinics to be full of serious people in starched white lab coats and green surgical scrubs doing serious things. I would only be in the way. I was comfortable in the biology lab. I was happy in the biology lab. I was really beginning to doubt whether this was a good idea.

But I tried again, and eventually I made it through all seven turns of the dial, literally sweating and shaking. A cheerful voice answered right away. "Of course," she said. "No problem. Come down any time. Rosemary loves students and could use a hand."

"Rosemary?" I thought. "The receptionist calls the veterinarian by her first name?" This was my first clue that my expectations were mostly out to lunch.

It was a sunny late spring day. I had the afternoon off from classes and labs and decided to go straight down. I was still very nervous, but the phone call had been the worst part, and once past it I felt a sense of elation that tempered my nervousness. It was a very small clinic with just two seats in the waiting room. There was nobody there. Not only were there no clients, but there was nobody behind the front desk. I stood there for several long moments, unsure of what to do, my anxiety beginning to rise again. Then there was a loud noise from the back, like something metal falling, followed by an emphatic "Bugger!"

I was on the verge of slipping back out the door when a young woman appeared in the hall leading back from the front desk.

"Hi, you must be Philipp!"

"Yes, I am." I extended my hand. "Pleased to meet you."

"I'm Wendy. Your timing is perfect. Come right on back." She grabbed some sort of instrument from a cupboard in the hall and led me to the back, where there was a room with a metal table in the middle. There were crowded shelves along the walls and two doors leading out. A middle-aged woman in a t-shirt, cargo pants and flip-flops stood at the table, holding a long-haired orange cat.

"Rosemary, this is Philipp, our new student."

*This was the vet??*

The woman at the table smiled broadly and shook my hand. "Welcome, Philipp! Rosemary Miller." She had a strong Australian accent. "Now please come around over here. This is Tiger. Wendy's going to hold him while I get the sample. What I would like you to do is tickle his ears to distract him."

I had never tickled a cat's ears before, so I was concerned that I wasn't doing it correctly, but nobody commented, and Tiger seemed content enough.

When the procedure was done, Wendy took Tiger through one of the doors, which appeared to lead to a small kennel and storage area. Dr. Miller (I couldn't yet bring myself to think of her as Rosemary) kicked off one of her flip-flops, hoisted her foot onto the exam table and proceeded to cut her toenails while she chatted with me. "So next we're going to fix a cat's broken leg. You can watch the surgery and then help with the recovery."

"OK." The pace of surprises here, and the nature of those surprises, was making me lightheaded. Then I remembered to add, "Thank you."

Dr. Miller was intent on her other foot and laughed. "No worries!"

I soon learned that her husband lectured in human medicine at the university and that she had opened this clinic just for fun and for what she referred to as "pin money." The hours were erratic and eccentric, and often it was quiet, and we just sat around and chatted, but when animals did come in, the diversity of cases was astonishing. I came into Rosemary's clinic knowing absolutely nothing about small animal practice and left with the beginning of a sense that something was shifting inside me.

## HOGWARTS ON THE SOUTH SASKATCHEWAN

It would be a simple matter to fill half this book with stories from my time at vet college, but I'm guessing that's not what you're here for. So instead allow me to summarize the experience in the broadest strokes by making a comparison that many of you are likely familiar with.

Should you ever find yourself in Saskatoon, you must make a point of visiting the University of Saskatchewan. It is widely considered one of Canada's prettiest universities with its leafy riverside setting and its hundred-year-old neo-Gothic limestone-clad buildings clustered around a lovely central green. And while you're there, please wander over to the northeast corner of campus, past the Physics building, towards the College of Agriculture, where the more modern buildings squat in exile. There you'll see it. Just past the grey cement bunker of the College of Engineering you will see a castle. You will have to squint a little, and you will have to use your imagination a little, but take note of the bridge, and of the turrets and of the asymmetrical wings. It is a castle, a modern castle. And, in my view, it is not just any castle. In my view this is what Hogwarts Castle would look like had it been designed by the mid-century modernist architect Le Corbusier.* This castle is actually the Western College of Veterinary Medicine (WCVM).

At this point in the story I should offer a disclaimer. It doesn't matter at all if you have no idea who Le Corbusier is, but it probably does matter if you don't know what Hogwarts is, in which case you should probably stop reading here as the rest of this is not going to make any sense.

I came to Harry Potter later in life than many people,

---

* WCVM was not designed by Le Corbusier, but I mention him for those of you who know him so that you have approximately the right mental image.

courtesy of my daughter, so the resemblance between WCVM and Hogwarts only occurred to me recently. In fact, as it happens, J.K. Rowling had her famous inspiration on that delayed train from Manchester to London at almost the exact same time as I was graduating from vet college, so the stories weren't written yet when I was there. Once I made the connection, though, I realized that it's not just the vaguely castle-like exterior that evokes Hogwarts. The interior has dungeons (pathology and necropsy labs), a great hall (the cafeteria), dark labs and lecture halls, curious things floating in jars and set on dusty display shelves, skeletons mounted on pedestals, a mazelike layout, several confusing winding staircases, a remote headmaster's (dean's) office in a tower, strange smells and sounds and a library with a separate mezzanine level that resembles the restricted section of the Hogwarts library.

As soon as I had this epiphany, several other pieces rapidly fell into place. It felt a bit like looking at that optical illusion where, depending on your perspective, it can either be a young woman looking away or an old hag looking down. I had been seeing the old hag all my life, and then suddenly I saw the young woman.

Pharmacology class was Potions. Animal Science was Care of Magical Creatures (Care of Agricultural Creatures) and I suppose Parasitology was also Care of Magical Creatures. Toxicology was Herbology. Small Animal Medicine was Charms. Anaesthesia was Defence Against the Dark Arts. And Clinical Pathology was Divination. Clearly, we had some classes that weren't offered at Hogwarts (Large

Animal Surgery, Immunology, Histology, etc.) and vice versa (Flying, Transfiguration and History of Magic come to mind), but the parallels are still striking given that one school was turning out veterinarians and the other witches and wizards. In retrospect, even the faculty and staff were eerily similar with their idiosyncrasies and strong personalities. And there were more than few with English or Scottish accents.

Hogwarts students (and fans) are sorted into four houses,* while WCVM students come pre-sorted from the four western provinces. I haven't worked out all the equivalents, but Manitoba is clearly Hufflepuff. Even the fact that the great majority of the students are from elsewhere, often away from home for the first time, sets WCVM apart from the other university colleges and puts it more in line with the Hogwarts experience. In my year only four students were from the city of Saskatoon itself. Although most students didn't actually sleep in the building (note — I said "most"), we all felt like we essentially lived there, and many did live together nearby, sharing rent.

And then when you graduate you feel like you belong to an obscure and semi-secret separate society. There is an arcane lore, a special language, specific skills, weird knowledge and, at times, an air of mystery when viewed from the outside. When you meet other veterinarians, there is an immediate feeling of kinship, of sharing something that outsiders will never really understand. And honestly,

---

* I am apparently in Ravenclaw.

sometimes the rest of you seem like Muggles to us. But I say that with abundant respect and affection. Most of us are far more Arthur Weasley than Lucius Malfoy.

That is the very last I will mention of Harry Potter. I promise. You can safely keep reading this book.

# SO YOU WANT TO BE A VETERINARIAN

Veterinarians love animals. This is a fundamental axiomatic truth, much like pilots loving airplanes, chefs loving food and librarians loving books. Given that the love of animals is widespread, the ambition to become a veterinarian is widespread as well. This spawns tremendous competition for the few spots in the veterinary schools, meaning that very high marks are required to get in. Consequently, and quite logically, it is animal lovers with excellent grades who populate the ranks of future veterinarians. But sometimes a third essential ingredient is missing. In fact, this ingredient is rarely even discussed, but it is the one element that more than any other determines whether these keen and idealistic students ultimately become happy veterinarians who maintain some of that keenness and idealism, or whether they become disillusioned veterinarians who burn out and succumb to cynicism and regret.

That third essential ingredient is a love of people. The same high marks would easily get any prospective veterinary student into human medical school, but for many this is ruled out not just by the pull of their love for animals but, unfortunately, by the push of their, shall we say, discomfort around people. This is a problem. I tell every prospective veterinary student that comes through our clinic that veterinary medicine is not an animal business that happens to involve people, but a people business that happens to involve animals. I tell them that the sooner they understand this, and accept this and embrace this, the sooner they will come to love their profession.

And why is that? The answer should be obvious. Until the dogs and cats and guinea pigs and rabbits and all others come marching in on their own equipped with the ability to talk (and pay), we will have to work through their owners and keepers and guardians. You can only help animals by communicating clearly and empathetically with people. Moreover, even when this miraculous Dr. Dolittle day arrives, we will still have staff to deal with. And staff are most assuredly people.

I have been chair of our professional disciplinary body for a number of years and can attest without a flicker of hesitation that far, far more veterinarians come to grief through an inability to connect with people than through any failings in their surgical skills or medical knowledge.

And once you "get it," you see how fabulously interesting people are in all their freakish variety. And you see that we are in a privileged profession as we are permitted to help people who are ironically often at their most human around animals. I remember with startling clarity the specific moment when this dawned on me. I was just about to enter the clinic through the back door. It was a sunny summer morning, and as I opened the door I realized for the first time that I was looking forward to seeing the clients who were starting to become my regulars as much as I was looking forward to seeing their pets. It was at this moment that I decided to stay in practice and not go back to school to pursue research, which had been my original plan.

But all that said, the love of animals is still at the heart of things. I often think of a card we got many years ago from a young child who boldly wrote, "I want to be a vat!" Yes, I too once aspired to be a large container, but I became an animal doctor instead, and I have never regretted that decision.

# PART 2

# THE ART OF
# VETERINARY MEDICINE

## A MILE WIDE

When people say that it must be harder to be a veterinarian than an MD, they often make two observations. The first is that our patients don't talk. (As an aside, this is actually not always a bad thing. It's difficult enough to sort through contradictory information from a husband and a wife without the cat talking too.) The second observation is that we have to deal with so many different species. This is correct for the profession as a whole, but in truth there aren't very many James Herriot *All Creatures Great and Small** types around

---

* His best-known book, widely referred to among veterinarians as *All Creatures Grunt and Smell*.

anymore. More and more of us restrict our practices to a handful of species. Which is of course still more than one.

However, what people often don't consider, and what is truly difficult (but fun), is the range of what we can do. Physicians are usually limited to family practice or a specific specialty, whereas as a veterinarian in general practice, I am a "family doctor," an internist, a general surgeon, a dentist, an anaesthesiologist, a radiologist, a behaviourist, a nutritionist, an oncologist, a cardiologist, an ophthalmologist, a dermatologist, a pharmacist, an obstetrician, a pediatrician, a gerontologist and a bereavement counsellor.

I am a mile wide.

And, as the aphorism goes, unfortunately sometimes (often?) just an inch deep. To be fair, the depth does vary. Most of us are deepest in the general medicine, internal medicine and general surgery categories and then have a handful of other areas of interest where our depth exceeds the proverbial inch. Three things save us from malpractice in the shallow zone:

1) Colleagues. Veterinarians, as a rule, get along well together, and veterinarians, as a rule, know their own limits. Strengths and weaknesses tend to balance each other out within a group of veterinarians working together, so cases are discussed and shared. And when this is not enough, or for those in solo practice, referral to specialists or to colleagues in other practices with particular training, experience or equipment is common.

2) Continuing Education. In order to maintain our licence, we have to attend conferences where new information is presented and where refresher courses are offered. I was just at a conference in Florida last week for exactly that reason. Sure, Philipp, a "conference" in Florida . . . in February . . . how convenient. OK, we did tack on a holiday after, but honestly, during the conference time the warmth and sunshine outside were an abstraction when considered from the artificially lit, aggressively air-conditioned interior of massive lecture halls. But it was fun! For you youngsters out there, here's a fact that may surprise you: learning is big fun when there are no exams or assignments or pressures of any sort. One lecture in particular caught my attention and made me laugh: "Hippopotamus Medicine Made Easy." Sadly I couldn't justify going to it, but it is an excellent illustration of how broad our profession is.

3) The Internet. There, I said it out loud and publicly. Vets look stuff up on the internet. However, I don't mean the wide-open internet, but specifically the Veterinary Information Network, or as we all call it, "Vin." Vin is a lifesaver — literally, for some of my patients — and it is something other professions are jealous of. It's an online subscription service that allows us access to scores of specialists to whom we can post questions on open forums. It also has

an impressive array of tools and resource materials and, as it has been running for about 15 years, it now has such a massive searchable database of past questions that I am often hard pressed to think of anything new to ask. Here's a secret: when your pet has something odd and your veterinarian pops out of the room for any reason or excuse, chances are they are also quickly logging into Vin.

Being wide keeps things interesting. Being shallow keeps things scary. As with most things in life, the key is in getting the balance right. And in leaving the hippos to the specialists.

## THE NAMING

One of the unsung minor perks of being in small animal practice is the exposure to the ever-changing landscape of pet names. This might not seem like a true perk, but I enjoy learning the names and, for the unusual ones, asking their owners how they came up with them. For obvious reasons people allow themselves far more latitude for creativity with their pets' names than with their children's. That said, there is also a lot of overlap, and there has been more than one family where I have had to be very careful not to refer to the dog by the daughter's name because, honestly, Bailey is a far more common dog name than human name (with all due respect to you wonderful human Baileys out there).

The range of pet names is breathtaking. I normally change all the names in the blog, but for the purposes of this discussion, I'm sure nobody will object if I just list the names of all the animals I saw at work yesterday as an example of what I mean: Tikka, Snerkle, Junie, Gunner, Silvester, Kayne, Kirby, Annabell, Maggie, Milkshake, Poppy, Stewie, Ben, Wimbley, Rico and Castle. This is absolutely typical. Nothing too wild, but clearly a lot of thought and some creativity there. And each of them an individual suited to their name.

Some common names are presumably easy and quick to think up — Tigger for a tabby cat, Blackie for a black Labrador — but many probably involved a lot of debate in the family. For those of you for whom this was the case, isn't it interesting how a name that was so difficult to come up with, and that you were a bit uncertain about at first, now seems so inevitable and perfect in retrospect? This even happens for objectively inappropriate names. I had a cat patient named Bob for a number of years. Bob was a girl. Bob's owners had been told that she was a he when they got him/her, and they didn't think to double-check. I had to break the news to them when they brought Bob in for her first shots, at which point the name had already stuck. They didn't try to feminize it to Bobbie or Roberta, saying that she still "looked like a Bob." And you know what? They were right. I now can't imagine her being called anything else.

My own dog's name of Orbit came about after trying on several others that just didn't feel right. One day we were watching him rocket around the house in circles, and we started saying Sputnik. Yeah, I know, that would have been wrong in so many ways, but it did get us going on that theme, from which Orbit emerged. It also helped that he ate everything in sight, and that roadside trash containers in Manitoba when we were growing up were called "Orbit," as in "Put your trash in Orbit!" Our one cat, Lucy, was named by my daughter after a second cousin in Germany who had made a strong impression on her. We got the second cat shortly after, and Isabel thought she should have a German human name as well. For fairness and symmetry, you know. Many were considered and rejected until she settled on Gabriella, which instantly became Gabi.

But of course the best part of discussing pet names are the weird ones and the funny ones. Unfortunately, although my memory is generally really very good, it has a glitch when it comes to names. They appear to reside in the mental equivalent of a sock drawer. So while I originally intended to present something like a "Top 20 Fun and Wacky Pet Names I Have Encountered," sitting here right now I can only come up with three.

In no particular order, then:

1) Russell Bertrand — As in, the cat's name was Russell, and the owner's last name was Bertrand.

The fact that this amuses me speaks strongly to my geekiness. The reverse, Bertrand Russell, was an important English philosopher, writer and Nobel Prize winner who lived from 1872 to 1970. The best part is that the owners seemed unaware of this coincidence and gave me a funny look when I laughed and said, "Ha! Russell Bertrand! That's great!"

2) Maximillian Samba-socks — Another cat. I don't know why, but this one still cracks me up years later. Even this bizarre name suited him perfectly. Maximillian Samba-socks could only be Maximillian Samba-socks.

3) Satan — They thought it was hilarious naming their little black poodle Satan. At least, they thought it was hilarious until they found out that he had a habit of disappearing deep into their big yard at night and often had to be loudly and repeatedly called back to the house: "Satan! Satan, come here!"

# MISMATCH

Among the more venerable internet memes are the photos of people who look like their pets. Or who allegedly look like their pets. Honestly, in most cases it seems to come down to some similarity in hair/fur and being photographed when they happen to have (or, more probably, have been coached to have) comparable facial expressions. Put a little wig on a potato, and you could just as easily come up with photos of people who look like their potatoes. That being said, there certainly are a few pudgy, flat-faced people with pudgy, flat-faced dogs, as there are a few tall, elegant people with long noses who have tall, elegant dogs with long noses. It is safe to say, however, that the overwhelming majority of people do not resemble their pets at all. And this, you'll agree, is a good thing.

What strikes me as far more interesting than owners who match their pets are owners who are wild mismatches for their pets, not only in appearance, but in temperament. It goes without saying that veterinarians see all kinds of combinations of animals and people, but the ones that really stick in our memories are the ones that seem the most improbable. I'll share two short stories with you about such mismatches.

The first pair is Tim and Mindy. Tim is the owner and Mindy is the dog. This is important to clarify because I can't count the number of times I have accidentally called the owner by their pet's name and vice versa. Consider yourself forewarned if you give your pet a conceivably human name. But I digress. Tim made a vivid first impression with his considerable size, his forceful handshake, his loud, expletive-laden style of talking and the impressive array of smudgy blue tattoos that looked suspiciously like they had been done in prison. But, as we all know, first impressions can be misleading. Two facts immediately emerged that ran counter to that impression. First of all, Tim turned out to be very friendly and very eager to learn everything he could about looking after his pet. And second of all, Mindy was a small, quiet female Shih Tzu who sported pink bows in her beautifully groomed fur. There were no pink bows anywhere on Tim. Nor was he especially beautifully groomed. They did not resemble each other in the slightest. In fact, they could have been considered polar opposites.

Tim was a long-distance truck driver, and Mindy was his companion on the road. "Been with me to 43 states and eight provinces!" It appeared that Mindy was his only family as well. To see Tim transform instantly from brash and boisterous with me to tender and calm with her was as astonishing as it was heart-warming. Utterly unselfconscious, he would gently and repeatedly kiss Mindy on the top her head while I explained something to him. Almost everybody loves their pets, but Tim's devotion to Mindy was in a category of its own. All of us adults know by now that love is a strange thing that cannot be predicted or judged. This was a prime example of that truth.

I typically saw Mindy once a year in the early spring for a check-up and to make sure that her shots and paperwork were in order for her frequent border crossings. Tim was also one of the few clients who insisted on regular blood work to follow baselines on her organ functions. He explained that he wanted the peace of mind and pressed me about whether there was anything else we could do to ensure Mindy's health. He gave up smoking when he got

Mindy because he was worried about second-hand smoke, and he planned his rest stops around where it was best to walk her. I said he was devoted, and I meant it.

You might be girding yourself for a heartbreaking ending to this story, but fortunately, to the best of my knowledge, Mindy remains healthy as I write this, and I expect to see her again next year. One day there may be an anguished phone call from Alabama or Arizona, but it hasn't happened yet, and, I tell you, I don't even want to think about it.

The second mismatched pair is Mrs. Abrams and Max. Max was a German shepherd. Actually, "Max" is almost always a German shepherd, unless he is a Boxer or a black cat. I picked this pair for the second story because it is in many ways the inverse of Tim and Mindy. Mrs. Abrams was small, quiet, elderly and fragile looking. Max, on the other hand, was large and loud and rambunctious. He weighed as much as Mrs. Abrams, if not even a little more. Her son had given him to her for protection. I suppose this was effective as Max would lunge and bark furiously whenever someone other than Mrs. Abrams moved towards him. Actually, he would lunge and bark furiously whenever the wind blew a scrap of plastic towards him as well. Fortunately he was a classic example of the bark being worse than the bite, and there was no need to be afraid of him, but unfortunately all that lunging made walking him dangerous for Mrs. Abrams.

One day she came in sporting a cast on her wrist. Max had pulled her down again. Apparently he had seen a particularly irritating squirrel. Mrs. Abrams always excused his behaviour with a chuckle and a "dogs will be dogs." After I addressed the rash that he had been brought in for, I talked to her about safer options for walking him. I had talked to her about this before, about halter types of collars and training methods, but the answer was always the same. In her soft voice she would say, "Oh no, he wouldn't like that." And that was the end of the discussion. What Max liked and did not like was always the decisive factor.

Eventually it came out that Max was also pooping in the house. Here too excuses were made and any type of training that would inconvenience Max in any way was dismissed out of hand. She would smile at Max like all the light in the world emanated from him. Like with Tim and Mindy, this was clearly also love, and love like that should not be judged, but my God, it was hard not to judge. Max was so manifestly the wrong pet for her. Wrong size, wrong temperament, wrong breed, wrong everything. But she felt safe with him, and she loved him with all her heart, and these two things obviously made broken wrists and poopy carpets seem like trifling inconveniences to her.

When Max eventually passed away, I didn't think I'd see Mrs. Abrams again. She seemed incalculably ancient, and there sadly comes a time in many people's lives when looking after an animal is just too difficult. I was surprised, then, to hear that she had booked an appointment with a new pet. Perhaps a cat, I thought, or a little Yorkie? Nope. Another German shepherd. Also named Max.

## SUPERSONIC OCTOPUS

*June 1.*

First receptionist: "Philipp, Mrs. Patterson is late, can I set up Mr. Cho instead?"

"Uh, sure." I'm trotting down the hall, hoping to get to my computer to catch up on files.

Then it occurs to me. "Mr. Cho? I don't remember seeing him in the schedule."

"No, he's a squeeze-in. Killer collapsed, and he says 'stuff is coming out of him'!"

"Oh, OK." I turn around and head to the exam room.

Second receptionist: "Mrs. Patterson just showed up. She apologizes, it was the traffic, but she has to see you today. And your next appointment is here too. They're a bit early."

"OK, well I'll look in quickly on Killer, and then I'll see Mrs. Patterson's dog."

First technologist: "Philipp, can you come into the back? I think Dodo is having a seizure."

Third receptionist: "Can you pick up the phone first, please? Mrs. Wilson says she has left three messages and needs to talk to you right now before they leave for the cottage."

"Um."

First receptionist, back again: "Before you see Cho and Patterson, the Samsons are here to pick up those prescriptions you told them you'd have ready."

First colleague: "Philipp, can you squeeze in an ultrasound soon? I think Buzz Firth is bleeding internally."

Second technologist: "Buzz's owners are here now visiting him and want to know what's going on. Did you do that ultrasound yet?"

Second receptionist again: "I set up Mrs. Patterson, she brought her other dog too, hoping that after you see Bruce for his chronic diarrhea, you'd have time to discuss Brent's chronic skin condition, which has gotten a lot worse." (Yes, a pair of cockers named Bruce and Brent.)

Third receptionist again: "Before you talk to Mrs. Wilson, can you quickly answer a question from your last appointment? Mr. Schmidt's at the counter still and has his wife on the phone, who reminded him what he was supposed to ask."

I haven't checked phone messages in two hours. I haven't written on files in three hours. I haven't been to the bathroom since I got to work. Then my brain begins to liquefy, and I slump into a gibbering heap on the floor.

OK, that last bit isn't true. Not exactly. And the very first line is misleading too — June 1 is truly the epicentre of our ultra-busy heartworm season, but I'm not at the clinic today. Today is my day off. Today I am mowing the lawn, drinking beer and writing this.

When the kids were small and they would pepper me with a series of complex overlapping requests, I would joke with them that I was not a "supersonic octopus." This expression comes back to me frequently this time of year.

A PUBLIC SERVICE ANNOUNCEMENT POSTSCRIPT
It is critical that you give your dog heartworm prevention medication. However, it is *not critical* that you give the first dose right on June 1 (or whenever is recommended in your region). Please do not phone your clinic in a panic today or tomorrow. As long as the first dose is given within a month or so of the first mosquito bite, it will still work well. The medications kill the first larval stages of heartworm in the bloodstream before they can do any harm.

❧ ❧ ❧

# AN OPEN LETTER TO THE CLIENT IN THE PARK WHOSE NAME I FORGOT

Dear Client,

It will come to me. Just give me a little longer and it will come to me. But in the meantime, I do apologize. It was clearly awkward for both of us. You saying a friendly and hearty "Hi, Dr. Schott!" and me saying an I hope equally friendly, but unfortunately slightly less hearty "Hi . . . !"

I recognized you for sure. I just couldn't remember your name. Or that of your pet. Or pets. Or their species. Or whether they were still alive. So I had to substitute, "How's [insert name of pet(s) here] doing?" with "How are you?" which is OK, but not as good. I wish you had had your dog(s) with you. That would have helped jog my memory. Should that have been a clue? Maybe you don't have dogs.

But the awkward bit was when it was obvious after you stopped to chat that I should introduce my family. This is when I could tell from your face that you realized I didn't remember your name. You're a kind and understanding person, so you weren't hurt or disappointed; rather you felt bad that you'd put me in the position of having to try to remember. And I felt bad that you felt bad on top of the feeling bad that I couldn't remember. And now you probably feel bad that I felt bad that . . . never mind.

So here's the thing. I'm sure that you are smart in addition to being kind and understanding, so you know this already, but it still bears explaining. The thing is that you have a box in your brain marked "veterinarian" and another marked "dentist" and another marked "piano teacher" and so on. Each of these boxes contains one, or perhaps at most a handful, of names and faces. Pretty straightforward to connect those names and faces. I have a box in my brain marked "clients." It contains upwards of 6,000 names and faces. I have a decent memory, but . . . well, you get it.

What you might not get, though, is that you don't even necessarily want to be one of the names I can connect to faces. Just like with a newspaper, where far more bad news gets printed than good, far more names connect to faces when they are associated with something bad. It's just more memorable.

So if I do remember your name, it often means one of two things: that you are one of those wacky clients staff talk about all the time, or that your pets are way too sick way too often.

In other words, you should feel really good that I didn't remember your name. But give me a bit more time and I will remember. It's on the tip of my tongue. Just like when you're trying to remember that actor who was in that movie with what's-her-name who used to be married to what's-his-name in that other movie, you know? Right? Yes, that one.

Once again, my apologies.

Sincerely,

Dr. Philipp Schott, BSc, DVM

# PLEASE REPEAT THAT IN ENGLISH

Every veterinarian gets this from time to time. We have just finished painstakingly explaining a complex medical condition to a client and then, after a brief silence, the client says, "Please repeat that in English!"

We have failed to communicate clearly. We have used jargon, or at least we have used words that didn't seem like jargon to us, but clearly seemed that way to the client.

Why does this happen? Three reasons:

1) When we are first starting in practice, we sometimes use big words and convoluted explanations to demonstrate our knowledge and win the client's trust in our competence. I looked very young when I graduated in 1990. I got called Doogie Howser a lot (the reference itself tells you how long ago that was). Consequently, I tried to impress with Latin. Look, I really am a doctor! I don't do that anymore. I don't need to. Now I get called "the old guy." I'm undecided which is better.

2) We don't want to insult clients by dumbing it down. In reality only peculiar people are insulted, and there is no pleasing them anyway. Most clients who prefer that you use more technical language will politely tell you so, and often

be pleased that they have the opportunity to tell you so.

3) We have "the curse of knowledge." This is the big one and the hardest one to overcome. A few years ago a Stanford University researcher conducted an experiment wherein she asked people to tap out the rhythm of a well-known song, like "Happy Birthday" or "Mary Had a Little Lamb," and then asked other people to guess what the song was based on the tapping. The tappers predicted that the listeners would guess correctly 50% of the time. In reality only just over 2% of the listeners did! The tappers had the curse of knowledge. It is impossible for them not to hear the tune in their minds while tapping, and — here is the key point — it is almost as impossible for them to be able to imagine someone not hearing the same thing in their minds. Once you know something, it is very difficult to recreate the state of mind that existed when you didn't know it.

So veterinarians can no longer put themselves in the minds of people who don't know the difference between a colon and a duodenum, or between an antibiotic and an anti-inflammatory or, my favourite, between the abdomen and the stomach. We're not alone though. All professionals do this. Actually, all people with specialized knowledge do. Car mechanics and accountants are the worst in my experience.

What can we do about this? If we have certain regular spiels, we should try them out on our unsuspecting family members or friends. And we should try to put ourselves in that unknowing frame of mind as often as possible. For my part, I am trying to learn to play the mountain dulcimer (yeah, yeah, whatever), and whenever my musical friends start talking about "in the key of . . ." and "quarter tones" and whatnot, they have the curse of knowledge, and I feel like the drooling guy in the wool cap who delivers the flyers. This make me humble. This gives me empathy, and empathy is a key ingredient in effective communication.

I'll close with an illustrative anecdote. A few years ago an elderly lady came in with a little white fluffy dog. We'll call her Mrs. Winterbottom and the dog Priscilla. Mrs. Winterbottom was a very elegantly dressed woman with a lovely summer dress, matching shoes, a matching handbag and even a matching hat. She spoke very properly and politely.

"Mrs. Winterbottom, we're going to need to run a fecal on Priscilla."

Blank look.

"I'd like to do a stool test."

Still blank.

"Um, so, do you think you can collect one of her . . . um . . . bowel movements?"

Dawning comprehension and a big smile. "You mean bring her shit!"

Indeed. I think I'll stick with "bowel movement."

# WHY HASN'T THE DOCTOR
# CALLED ME BACK YET?

My father was dying of brain cancer. He had a glioblastoma removed from his left prefrontal cortex and was given months to live. He was a professor, and his intellectual capabilities were unimpaired, but his judgment and social graces, such as they were, had been annihilated. Told by the surgeon that they had removed the tumour using suction, my father delighted in pointing to the large scar on his forehead and loudly telling strangers that his brain had been removed by a vacuum cleaner. There were other surprising moments of levity, but otherwise this was a bleak time. He was too young for this, and we were not ready to lose him. Not nearly.

A few weeks after the surgery an issue arose regarding one of his medications. I don't recall which or why, but I do recall being quite anxious about it. It was not an emergency by any stretch, but the problem was beginning to spiral in our minds, so I phoned his oncologist to ask about it. He was unable to come to the phone, so his receptionist took a message. Ten minutes went by, then twenty, thirty, forty, fifty . . . By the time a full hour rolled around, I had checked twice to make sure the phone was working (dial tone? yes.) and my pacing had become obsessive. I couldn't read, I couldn't listen to music, I couldn't concentrate on chores. I couldn't think about anything except a recursive loop of "Why hasn't he called me back yet!?!?"

"Why?!?!?"

"It would only take a minute!"

At the two-hour mark, my tone had darkened. I was much quicker to anger in those days. "I can't effing believe this! He can't find a minute to help a dying man?"

"The arrogant prick!!"

I was beside myself. I left another message, trying to make my voice sound like cold steel, gleaming with sarcastic fury. But at least another hour passed before he called. When he did his tone was disarmingly pleasant and empathetic. He took the time needed to properly answer my questions, and the problem was sorted.

All these many years later I still cringe when I think of how I reacted that day. I cringe in part in recognition of the different person I was then, and I cringe in part imagining how my own clients must sometimes feel when I am slow returning their calls. I know that most people are reasonable and understanding, but I know that some must be just like I was: in a vulnerable and slightly irrational emotional state, or perhaps just unaware of the workflow in a busy clinical setting.

So, for the latter group, it is probably worthwhile explaining the "type of busy" that we often are. In some jobs you can be very busy doing one thing. You have a single important task in front of you that is fully occupying your time, but you can take regular breaks from it to quickly address other matters as they arise. Veterinary (and presumably human medical) practice is not like that. We generally have numerous simultaneous demands on our attention throughout our entire shift. We are constantly in triage mode, figuring out in what order to do things so that the least number of people with urgent problems are left waiting the least amount of time. Moreover, for telephone messages specifically, in some cases it may be a few hours before we even *see* the message, let alone try to fit it into our triage. Another factor is that estimating the length of a phone call is notoriously difficult, for both the client and the doctor, so we are sometimes unwilling to take the risk of being drawn into a long conversation and will leave it until a gap opens in our schedule or to the end of our shift. This is almost certainly what happened with my father's oncologist. It was closer to ten minutes than one, and he was wise enough to leave it for the end of his day.

So, in the interest of reducing stress for both parties, here is "How to Contact Your Veterinarian":

By all means, please phone if you have any questions.

If you feel the question is urgent, tell the receptionist so.

Ask for a realistic guesstimate on when you are likely to hear back.

Please make sure the receptionist knows which phone number you can be reached at. Many files list multiple work and cell numbers for multiple family members in addition to the home landline.

Please make sure you specify if there are times you will not be available to be called back.

Please use email sparingly and only if you are OK with

waiting for a day or two for a response. Sometimes we're quick with email, but sometimes we're not. For a variety of practical reasons it is not given a high priority.

### THE LONESOME ZEBRA

Eddie pants nervously as I part his fur and examine the lump that Mr. Williamson is concerned about. I'm about to comment on it when Mr. Williamson asks the inevitable question: "Have you seen something like this before?"

To which I reply, "Yes, I have. Many times. Daily in fact. But that doesn't mean much." And then I explain myself briefly. But as you and I have a lot more time right now, and as you are presumably more interested in these things than the average person, I will explain myself at much greater length here.

It begins with the fact that humans are excellent at pattern recognition. This is largely a good thing, and it is one of the reasons our distant ancestors were able to avoid being eaten on the savannahs of Africa. Our brains are strongly wired to match everything new we encounter with past experience, whether consciously or unconsciously. That particular type of rustle in the tall grass? Could be a lion. Better keep quiet and slowly retreat.

However, in medical diagnosis, pattern recognition is

a problem. Some symptoms are what we call pathognomonic, meaning that they are specific to one particular disease, but the great majority are not. A red eye can be due to dozens of conditions. Coughing has scores of causes. And poor appetite can quite literally have hundreds of explanations. In veterinary school they try to beat pattern recognition out of us and replace it with a "problem-oriented" diagnostic process. I won't explain what that is. Trust me that it is as boring as it is important.

Eddie's lump is small, loose under the skin, smooth in contour and slightly rubbery in firmness. Pattern recognition dictates that this is almost certainly a lipoma, which is a benign fatty growth. But only "almost certainly." Eddie has never had one before — most dogs with lipomas have several — so I am wary of falling into that trap as a type of cancer called a mast cell tumour can feel very similar. I suggested collecting a few cells with a needle. Eddie was good for this as he was far more worried that I might be planning to trim his nails, which he hates more than anything in life. The needle aspirate just produced fat cells, so thankfully it was a benign lipoma.

So what about the zebra advertised in the title of the essay? I apologize if you read this hoping for a wacky patient story, but no, nobody has consulted me about their zebra problems. Which is a good thing. Instead I am referring to an old aphorism taught to every medical and veterinary student, which highlights the flip side of this issue: "When you hear hoofbeats, think of horses not zebras." In other words, although a set of symptoms *could* be the result of a bizarre rare disease, the common diseases are far more, well, common. Just as horses are far more common than zebras. Consequently, veterinarians have to exercise some balance and judgment and avoid freaking pet owners out with a laundry list of horrible possibilities accompanied by a wildly expensive diagnostic program.

Balance. Judgment. Tricky things. Don't obsess about the zebras, but don't ignore them either.

## BE KIND TO YOUR VETERINARIAN

I came into this profession because of the animals, and I have stayed because of the people. Not because the animals have become any less enjoyable — far from it — but because the people have become more enjoyable. Or perhaps more accurately, my capacity to enjoy the people has improved. Regardless, it is the interaction with clients that makes or breaks most veterinary careers. So in aid of this, here is a list of the top seven ways clients can be kind to their veterinarian and improve that key interaction (listed from silliest to most serious):

1) Please do not talk to me while I am using the stethoscope. It is a listening device. I cannot listen

to two things at once and make reasonable sense of either. One plus one equals zero. For the play-along-at-home version, try following what your friend is quietly saying on the telephone while your toddler simultaneously tries to tell you a story about a problem in the bathroom.

2) Please do not take personal offence if I tell you that your pet is overweight. A client once threatened to punch one of my partners for saying this. It is merely a statement of objectively measurable fact. I am not judging you. I have a volleyball-shaped cat. I get it.

3) Please avoid introducing multiple chronic medical concerns in an appointment you have booked for a simple ear check. My schedule is generally full, and the receptionist has booked enough time for you for what she understood the visit to be about. Normally I am delighted to discuss the multiple chronic medical concerns, but we do need warning at the time of booking so that enough time is set aside. The domino effect of falling behind because of this can turn a pleasant day (sunshine! bunnies! roses!) into a hellish simulation of a combat zone (darkness! terror! chaos!).

4) Please do not show up at random hoping to catch me "when I have a minute" to ask me some questions. I never have a minute that is not scheduled (see above). And I am too polite to tell you that, so I will squeeze this conversation in and fall behind

in my appointment schedule (see above again). Please make an appointment, leave a phone message, or email if you have a non-urgent question.

5) Please do not ask me why I can't figure out what's wrong with your pet moments after you've declined most of the tests I've recommended. For every set of symptoms and physical exam findings, there are dozens of possible causes. My crystal ball is broken today. In fact, it is broken every day, and I see little chance of it being fixed any time soon.

6) Please do not confuse anecdotes with statistics. Making decisions about your pet's health based on anecdotes would be like me taking up heavy drinking and smoking because my grandfather drank an entire bottle of wine by himself every day and smoked steadily and lived in great health to 93 years of age (a true story, actually). So when I say, "Vaccinations are proven to be very effective at preventing disease" (statistic), do not reply with "Our farm dogs never had shots and they got pretty old" (anecdote). Statistics get a bad rep when they are used to mislead, but without them we'd still be chanting and sacrificing chickens whenever anything went wrong.

7) Please do not bring me your pet when you've already made up your mind to euthanize, telling me that you've "tried everything" when what you've actually done is "tried everything you and

your neighbour whose daughter used to work at a kennel could think of and everything on the first page of Google hits." Maybe I could have helped if you'd contacted me much earlier before things went this far, or maybe not. We'll never know now, will we? This makes me very sad.

And who wants to be sad?

Fortunately, the above applies to a small minority of clients, so I'm not sad very often. And I've never been punched by a client. And I only drink part of a bottle of wine.

# THE UGLY

### THE GOOD
Fluffy kittens, puppies who wag their whole hind ends, difficult cases solved, lives saved, tricky procedures mastered, grateful clients, happy staff, appointments all running on time and so much more. Did I mention fluffy kittens?

### THE BAD
Screaming cats, biting dogs, cases gone sideways, lives lost, procedures failed, angry clients, grumpy staff, running three appointments behind and so much more.

## THE UGLY

This is what I want to talk about today. Briefly. Briefly because it aggravates me too much. The Bad is part of what we signed up for, and honestly, it is swamped by the Good, so most of us shake off the Bad pretty easily. But we didn't sign up for the Ugly. The Ugly is clients who are not only angry, but who are unreasonable, disruptive and abusive.

In the past I might have slotted them under the Bad as generally these stressful encounters were face to face, more or less private and blew over quickly. Now these abusive clients take to social media and vet ratings sites to become trolls and give their venom a sustained public life online. This is thankfully extremely rare, but even one can have a dramatic impact on a veterinarian's peace of mind. These people generally have mental health issues, which most readers of their rants will spot, but nonetheless even the most ridiculous slander, once out there, will have some impact. I've been lucky, but a couple of my colleagues have been attacked this way recently.

Maybe eventually social media and ratings sites will find a way to weed this out, but in the meantime, if you like your veterinarian, the very kindest thing you can do is to go on Google, Facebook and VetRatingz.com and write positive reviews. And bring in a fluffy kitten. Or two.

# ALL THE WACKY PEOPLE

But it's time to lighten up. Fortunately, for every client who behaves in an ugly fashion, there is at least one who behaves in a wacky and ultimately harmlessly entertaining fashion. On my blog the most popular posts by far were the heaviest and darkest ones. I'm not sure what to make of that. It does not reflect the reality of practice, which is a daily teeter-totter of happy and sad, amusing and stressful, heavy and light.

As I've mentioned before, veterinary medicine may be fundamentally about animals, but it is also far more about people than you might expect. The world is full of all manner of interesting people, but it seems that the *most* interesting ones all own animals. This is why veterinarians make great dinner party guests. If you can prevent them from telling gross-out stories (oh, but the urge is so strong . . .), they often have some fantastic wacky people stories.

In no particular order, here are the inductees to my Wacky People Hall of Fame:

The young man who had his beloved ferret freeze-dried after death and mounted on the mantlepiece in what he described as a "heroic pose."

The elderly woman who kept an astonishingly detailed diary of her perfectly healthy cat's eliminations on reams of loose leaf and then would proceed to try to read two months' worth aloud to me. "On March 13 he had one regular sized bowel movement at 6:03 in the morning and then . . ."

The man who missed his appointment because the bus driver wouldn't let him on. He had had his sick four-foot-long ball python draped around his shoulders.

The woman who phoned because she wanted me to talk to her canary. Not knowing how else to respond, I agreed. Once the bird had apparently been brought to the phone I said, "Hello, how are you?" in what can best be described as a tentative voice. There was some faint chirping on the other end of the line. The woman came back on, thanked me and hung up.

The woman who came to visit her dead dog the day after the euthanasia in order to groom him before the crematorium picked him up. He was a very large dog. She bathed him, shampooed him, blow-dried him and brushed him out, humming all along. It was deeply strange, but also heartrending.

The young woman who began to unbutton her pants, saying she wanted me to tell her whether the bites she had were from fleas. I declined, saying that all bug bites look the same.

The woman who brought her budgie in wanting to know why it wouldn't sing or eat. It was dead. Cue the Monty Python sketch . . .

The couple who were astonished to find out that their young cat was pregnant. "How could that happen? She doesn't go outside, and the only male around her is her brother!" (I'm sure every vet has run into this at least once.)

The woman who phoned and in a very high squeaky voice said, "I have always had the ability to smell cancer. All my friends say I can smell cancer. And I smell it on Billy. I want to bring him in so you can find it and get rid of it."

As for the last one, you may not want to read it aloud to the kids:

The woman who, with an entirely straight face, asked whether venereal diseases are transmissible between humans and dogs.

And at the end of it all, you should congratulate yourself that you are less wacky than you thought you were.

## THE ANATOMY OF A VET BILL

Mr. Malloy was the type of jovial older guy who wore a camouflage cap and red suspenders over an expansive gut. And the type of guy who loved cracking lame jokes. You know the type. Kind of annoying, yet also kind of lovable.

One day he was at the counter paying his bill when he said, "Holy Dinah! A hundred bucks? You gotta be kidding me? I must own a wing of this hospital by now!" At the other end of the counter, Mrs. Chung was paying her

$1,500 bill and quietly exchanging knowing smiles with the receptionist.

If we had a hospital wing for every client who felt they had paid for one, we would be the size of the Pentagon by now. (Besides, veterinary hospitals generally don't have "wings.") But I get it. For a lot of people, veterinary medicine is expensive.

Some in my profession push back against that statement and say that we just need to look at dentists' and plumbers' bills to see that we are not that expensive. No, dentists and plumbers are also expensive, just like us. A lot of modern life is expensive. For many people living paycheque to paycheque (47% of Canadians in 2017), a surprise $500 veterinary (or dental, or plumbing, or whatever) bill is difficult to manage, and a surprise $2,000 bill is a potential financial catastrophe.

So now that we have established that veterinary medicine is "expensive," let's focus on why it is expensive. The number one reason is that we have rapidly evolved to a point where our standards of care compare favourably to those for humans. The arguments about the rightness or wrongness and the whys and wherefores of this evolution are best left for another discussion, but the fact remains that we now practise close to "human-level" medicine and consequently have some "human-level" expenses. There are no special veterinary-grade sutures, catheters, pills, computers, rent or education for that matter. In fact, for many of our supplies we pay more as we don't have access to the volume discounts that human hospitals do. It is interesting to note that Americans complain about veterinary bills less often than Canadians because they know what human health care costs.

There are many scary expressions in a practice owner's lexicon — "audit," "lawsuit," "burst pipe," "crashed server" — but one of the scariest is "overhead." The others are avoidable, but overhead is unavoidable, and in some practices it can gobble up almost all of the revenue. In my clinic I have calculated that it costs us $400 an hour to keep the lights on, the doors open, the supplies stocked and the non-veterinary staff in place. This is before any veterinarian gets paid. During the busy season this is easy to cover, but in the doldrums of January, when you can hear the proverbial crickets in the waiting room, you may see me obsessively watching the bank balance and line of credit. I might even be chewing my fingernails.

So where does your money go? In our practice, on a very broad average, for every dollar you spend, about 25 cents covers veterinary salaries and benefits, 21 cents goes to staff salaries and benefits, 27 cents are for variable costs like drugs, supplies, lab charges, etc., and 15 cents go towards fixed costs like rent, computers, utilities, accounting, maintenance, etc. This obviously varies enormously from service to service, and it also varies a bit from year to year. Our veterinarians are on salary, so the 25 cents doesn't go straight to them, but in some practices vets are paid a percentage of their billings.

The mathematically astute among you will notice 12 cents missing. That is the theoretical profit, or, more accurately, return on investment, that is divided among the owners (there are seven in our practice) when we have kept a good eye on our overhead. Those of us who own practices have to take out substantial loans to buy them or, in the case of a new clinic, build them, so this money helps slowly pay those loans off. I suppose a theoretical non-profit clinic would be able to lower its prices by that 12% and would have to somehow fundraise to build, expand, etc. It would still be expensive. Veterinary medicine is expensive. But — and forgive the self-serving nature of this comment — it is so worth it. What price can you put on health and love? Especially in a world where people are apparently buying thousand-dollar smartphones.

## TABOO

It's the biggest taboo of all. Survey after survey indicates that people (North American people, at least) are more comfortable revealing details of their sex lives than details of their paycheques. For a variety of cultural and historical reasons, it is considered exceptionally rude to ask someone how much they earn. Yet people wonder.

I think most people believe that veterinarians are reasonably well paid, but not nearly as well as human doctors or dentists. And in broad strokes this is correct, so I could just stop there, but for those who are curious, I will lift the veil more completely. But first a short story.

We have all said things in the past that make us squirm with embarrassment when we think back on them. I have a veritable catalogue of such statements to draw on, but one in particular is relevant here. When I was a university student, I made one of my then-very-rare visits to the dentist. The dentist was a very pleasant fellow, and we had a good chat about summer plans (well, one of those dental-chair good chats where the dentist asks questions and I reply, "mm, mm, mhmm"). He really was a nice guy, and he did a good job. I don't recall specifically what was done or what the bill was, but I do vividly recall doing the math on how long I was in the chair and then declaring to my friends and anyone that would listen that this guy must clear $200 an hour (an insane amount in the 1980s)! I was an asshole. And I had done my math wrong — way wrong. Now, 30 years later, I know that "overhead," as explained in the last essay, is the 800-pound gorilla of the balance sheet. It would have gobbled up a very large chunk of his bill. I still feel bad for implying that he was gouging.

Fast forward to the present day, when a lot of my day is spent doing ultrasounds, which take around half an hour (although the client only sees 15 to 20 minutes of that as the rest is report writing) and cost around $300. Most people are not as ignorant as I was at 22, but I'm sure there are a few who walk out thinking, "This guy is making $600 an hour! Must be nice."

One zero too many. I earn $60 an hour.

Some clinics pay a percentage of billings, but we pay a straight salary to the doctors. It's an annual salary rather than a true hourly wage, so there is no overtime or anything like that. As far as I can tell, my salary is fairly typical for a small animal veterinarian in general practice with 28 years of experience. It's pretty close to the top end for a non-specialist. New graduates start in the $35 range.

A few of you are probably still thinking, "Sixty bucks an hour — must be nice!" It is nice, and I am not going to complain. But allow me to point out two important factors that make it perhaps less nice than it seems on the surface.

First of all, we put in six to eight years of university, where rather than working and earning money, we are generating debt. Lots and lots of debt. The median debt on graduation for veterinarians has grown dramatically to $65,000 now in Canada. In the US, it's $135,000!

And secondly, most of us do not have company or civil service pension plans. A significant amount of our income has to be diverted into retirement savings to make up for this. At least if we are able to, and if we are smart enough to.

In the interest of full disclosure, there is another potential income stream. Some of us, myself included, are also practice owners and earn money from any profit the practice might generate (most do generate some, but some don't). Here, however, there are also two important factors to take into account.

The first is that profit is not free money. Potential owners have to take out massive loans to buy into practices. This money could have been invested elsewhere, like in the stock market or bonds or real estate, but we have chosen to invest it where we work.

And secondly, I am part of a fortunate minority to have had the opportunity to buy into the practice. Younger veterinarians are having a harder time affording it because of the aforementioned debt load. Also, large corporations are increasingly buying practices, which prevents the doctors working there from ever becoming owners.

I know how lucky I am. It's not a life of luxury, but I never aspired to that, and it is a very good life. I have the trust of the thousands of pet owners who have come to me to thank for that. So, if you are one of those and are reading this, thank you!

## AT THE VERY HEART OF IT ALL

I've been in practice for a long time. When I'm asked what the biggest change has been over that time, I sit back, rub my chin thoughtfully, adopt my best wise old man tone, pause dramatically and then quietly say . . . "techs." Not all the new drugs — in 1990 we had hardly any pain medications we could send home. Not all the new in-house lab equipment — in 1990 we sent most samples away and waited a day or two for results. Not all the new diagnostic imaging equipment — in 1990 ultrasound was not generally available, and X-rays were developed in a dark-room with dip tanks of stinky chemicals. Not all the new dental equipment — in 1990 I used a hacksaw blade to cut apart large teeth that needed to be pulled. Not all the new knowledge, not all the new techniques, not all the new computerization. None of that. These things are important, crucial even, but the most pervasive change that has touched every aspect of veterinary practice is the role of the veterinary technologist (aka RVT, aka registered veterinary technologist, aka animal health technologist, aka veterinary nurse, aka tech).

To put it simply, since I began in 1990 techs have moved from being overqualified, underutilized animal holders and kennel cleaners to being at the very heart of almost every small animal practice. In 1990 many veterinarians simply trained people in house to perform whatever simple technical duties the veterinarian didn't want to do himself (and it was usually a himself, not a herself, in those days). The actual college-trained vet techs did very little more than these informal techs, which was a demoralizing and frustrating situation that contributed to a high rate of turnover and burnout. Looking back, it was a bizarre situation. As the veterinarian I took most of the blood samples, placed most of the IV catheters, took most of the X-rays, induced most of the anaesthetics and cleaned most of the teeth, even though the college-trained techs were perfectly qualified to do all of this. I was basically an expensive (although not that expensive in those days) tech for about half my job.

Today techs do practically everything except what the law reserves for veterinarians, which is diagnosing, prescribing and operating. In our practice, techs take every blood sample, place every IV, take every X-ray, induce every anaesthetic and perform every dental prophy and cleaning. Moreover, they command an in-house laboratory that looks like a miniature version of NASA Mission Control, they perform blood transfusions, they hook up ECGs, they monitor and care for critical hospitalized patients and they counsel clients on weight management, behaviour, post-operative care and a host of other subjects. And they do it all well. Very well. Each one is a medical nurse, an ICU nurse, an emergency nurse, a surgical nurse, a laboratory technologist, a nurse anaesthetist, a dental hygienist, an X-ray technologist, a neonatal nurse and a palliative nurse. All of that, and more.

In 1990 I could do absolutely everything in the clinic. I knew what every knob on every piece of equipment did, and I knew how to make it do that. I knew exactly how to get blood on every patient (well, almost every patient) and I could wield every instrument and administer every treatment. Today I am more or less useless. OK, I'm exaggerating for effect. More accurate is that I am useless without my techs. Absolutely useless and helpless.

Most clinics are designed with a large room in the centre called the treatment room. This is where all the action happens. It is the physical heart of the clinic with the laboratory, patient wards, anaesthetic prep area, operating room, pharmacy, dental area and X-ray suite radiating from it. And at the heart of this heart — at the very heart of it all — are the techs. Thank you, Jen, Kim, Mela, Brandi, Marnie, Melissa, Jamie and Jasmine. Thank you for making me so much less useless.

## CATS & DOGS & PARANOIA

It's dark and it's quiet in the house. It's dark and it's quiet because it is 2:00 a.m. I'm staring at the ceiling, which is pretty boring. I'm hoping that being bored will lull me back to sleep because, really, I would like to be sleeping at 2:00 a.m. I should be sleeping at 2:00 a.m. But you can't force yourself to be bored. My eyes might be bored, but not my brain. As soon as I woke up, some neuron somewhere in there began ringing the bell. I picture it like one of those old-fashioned "ring for service" brass bells. Sometimes I wake up and everything is quiet in brainland, and I drift back to sleep. But sometimes I wake up and a memory neuron starts hammering on the bell: "Ding! Ding! Ding! Ding! Stay awake! I've got something to tell you!" Tonight it was hollering, "You forgot to give that slide to the tech to send away! And it was so hard to get that sample from Callie! Mrs. Levesque is going to be so pissed when you tell her she has to bring that cat back in!"

Shit.

Callie was perhaps one of the top ten unhappiest cats in the practice. She could reliably be counted on to growl and hiss from inside the carrier the moment she came into the clinic. Sometimes she was even screaming from in there before we so much as looked at her. Mrs. Levesque had noticed a growth under the skin on her side. After a fair bit of wrangling with leather gloves and thick towels, I had managed to get a sample from the lump with a needle. I remembered transferring the sample to a glass slide in the exam room. And I remembered telling myself that once I was done talking to Mrs. Levesque, I should not forget to take the slide to the lab area for the techs to pack up to send out as this was something I thought a pathologist should look at. I remembered thinking that, but I did not remember actually doing it. Shit. Leaving the clinic that night, I'd had that funny sense that I was somehow forgetting something, but I couldn't put my finger on what it was. Now I knew. Shit shit. And to make matters worse, Pearl Levesque was one of those brusque, combative people who have a loudly articulated sense of right and wrong and who seem to constantly be on the lookout for the slightest misstep by anyone they deal with.

Shit shit shit.

I kept resolutely staring at the ceiling, trying to push these thoughts away and empty my mind. I wasn't having any luck. Other, more rational neurons kept pointing out that there wasn't anything I was going to be able to do about it at 2:00 a.m. anyway, but the bell-ringing neurons were louder and livelier. They must have eventually gotten exhausted, though, because at some point I did fall asleep again, fitfully dreaming anxious dreams.

I once read that psychologists divide people into two broad types: the neurotic and the character disordered. Faced with a problem, neurotics first ask themselves whether they might somehow be to blame and, moreover, they typically assume that the problem is worse than it actually is. Meanwhile character disordered people blame others, or downplay their role or the significance of the problem. My best guess is that 95% of veterinarians are neurotic. (I'll let you work out for yourself which professions are dominated by the character disordered.) I'm not really sure why this is, but it does help explain the high rates of burnout, substance abuse and even suicide.

I entered the clinic the next morning consumed by a sickening sense of dread. I was putting my coat away when one of the receptionists popped her head into the office. "Good morning, Philipp! That unlabelled slide you left in room three last night — I thought I better not throw it out, just in case. It's in the lab if you still need it."

I don't expect you to be happy if your vet makes a mistake, but before you get too mad, keep in mind that to err is indeed human, and that among humans, veterinarians are usually in the group most likely not to forgive themselves. So it would be great if you could do the forgiving, please.

## IN THE DARK

This is not a metaphor. I mean it literally. OK, I'll confess, sometimes it would be an appropriate metaphor, but
that's not what I'm writing about today. Today I'm writing
about the curious fact that I now spend roughly half my
time at work in a dark room.

After ten years in general small animal practice, I could
begin to see the rough outlines of burnout approaching
on the distant horizon, like a cloud of dust way down
a gravel road. I didn't know whether that cloud of dust
signified a puttering tractor or a careening semi-trailer
truck, but I didn't want to wait to find out. It wasn't anything I could put my finger on, just a growing sense that
I needed a different challenge. Don't get me wrong, general practice is extremely challenging, but it is made up
of thousands of individual challenges, case by case, that
keep you running like a proverbial hamster on a wheel.
But for me, there was increasingly no sense of progress on
something bigger.

At around that time we were starting to find more and
more uses for ultrasound, but no small animal veterinarians in Manitoba were doing it routinely, so we had to
get a human ultrasonographer who moonlighted going
from vet clinic to vet clinic with her portable machine. She
was great, but the limitations of that set-up were obvious.

Moreover, I found the technology fascinating, so whenever I had time, I would peer over her shoulder and annoy her by saying, "That's the liver, right?" and "What's that grey bit there? Beside the other grey bit?"

I was not a partner yet, so I approached my boss at the time with a proposal to buy an ultrasound machine for the clinic. It was a very big-ticket item, and even with creative math, I could not make a solid financial case for it, but Bob was a remarkably wise man and could both sense the implications to the practice of my restlessness and see beyond what the immediate numbers showed.

So in 2001 we bought an ultrasound machine, and I went to Calgary for a course. It was a revelation. Here was a world I could deep dive into that combined a fun technological toy with live anatomy, physiology and pathology, the subjects I had loved in school. Blood tests and urine tests and X-rays are cool in their own way, but they are static and removed and abstracted from the animal. Ultrasound was more like an extension of the physical exam. It was a live, real-time exploration of the interior of my patients. Another thing that excited me about ultrasound was how it was turning one of our weaker senses as a species, sound, into one of our stronger senses, vision. With ultrasound I was becoming like a dolphin or a bat and was seeing with sound. The hand–eye–brain coordination was going to take time to get consistently right, but the first few times that that grey mess on the screen automatically crystallized into a 3D organ in my mind were exhilarating. Furthermore, because it is done in a dark room, and because I drone on in a monotone, the animals were usually calm and the whole experience felt soothing and peaceful to me. I was hooked.

Over time I took more courses, in California and New York, but it became clear early on that the key to becoming proficient was caseload. You just had to practise a lot. It was more like learning to play a musical instrument or a new sport than anything else I had encountered in practice. So I began to set aside time to scan healthy patients who were in for spays and neuters. This also helped me build up a strong sense of what normal looked like, as well as how much variation there was within it.

And then the first referral came in. Another practice across town had heard I was doing this and wanted to send a patient over. I was terrified. I agreed on the condition that the pet owner understood that I was still learning. But it went well, and I failed to humiliate myself as expected. And then there were a few more referrals from that practice, and then some from a second practice, and then from a third and . . .

In the last 15 years I have done over 12,000 ultrasound studies for close to 40 clinics from southern Saskatchewan to northwestern Ontario. Now there are many veterinarians as well as an excellent human ultrasonographer doing it, but I am still busy enough with ultrasound that it takes up about half my time. And I still love it, and it is still helping keep the burnout at bay.

# BLACK COAT

Some days I feel like I should be wearing a black coat instead of a white one. Some days I feel like I am ending more lives than I am saving. Some days I really understand the people who tell me that they wanted to be a veterinarian until they learned that you have to euthanize pets.

Twenty-eight years in practice, and euthanasia is still the hardest thing I routinely do. I've gotten used to all manner of grim fluids and funky smells and chaotic days and wacky clients and freaked-out pets and hopeless cases, but I have not fully gotten used to euthanasia. Watching the light go out of an animal's eyes as their human companions dissolve into grief is not something that anyone should ever get used to, so it being hard will be a necessary and integral aspect of my job until I retire.

And it is a frequent part of my job as well. I think most of us average maybe two or three euthanasias a week. They tend to cluster, so sometimes I can end up performing three or four on a single day. Those are the black coat days. Most pets, probably 80–90%, die of euthanasia rather than of "natural causes" at home. If you think about it, it makes sense. How many people get to die in their beds at home? The majority of us will die in hospital or by slow degrees in palliative or chronic care facilities. There is no such place for a dog or cat to go once their quality of life is poor at home, and there is no longer any hope of it improving. There is no ward for demented pets to live out their last days, wearing a diaper, unable to walk, unable to feed themselves. There is only a reasonably good life at home, or death.

Seen this way euthanasia is of course, perhaps ironically, one of the best things we do as veterinarians. It allows us to fully focus on quality of life. No animal needs to suffer pointlessly the way some people do. It gives us a powerful tool many on the human side wish they had, if only they could find a clear path through the ethical minefield. We are still far more comfortable wielding the power of life and death over animals, but with that power comes responsibility, and with responsibility inevitably comes stress. It's just the way it is, and the way it must be.

It is interesting to note that I get far more thank you cards after euthanasias than after any other procedure. Far, far more. Some of this is thanks for service over the life of the pet, but some of it is also gratitude for the way the end of the pet's life was handled. It's funny, but veterinarians themselves are always most impressed by their colleagues' diagnostic and surgical skills, by the cool cases they've figured out and by the new treatments they've mastered. Clients never are. They just assume we know how to do all that stuff. What they are most impressed by is our compassion and caring, especially in those terrible emotionally fraught moments at the end of a pet's life.

But all that said, my heart still sinks every time I see a euthanasia booked for me and I have to don that black coat again.

## WHEN DARKNESS OVERWHELMS

*For Terry and Craig and Sophia*

This essay is going to be a departure from my usual lame attempt at a lighthearted tone (the last one aside). This essay is going to be about suicide in the veterinary profession. Statistics are not available for Canada, but in Britain two separate studies found the suicide rate among veterinarians to be four to six times that of the general population and double that of dentists and physicians. The American Centers for Disease Control did a survey of 10,000 veterinarians and found that a shocking one in six had considered suicide. I personally knew two colleagues here in Manitoba who took their own lives, and in 2014, a prominent and very well-liked behaviour specialist killed herself, drawing some media attention to this little-known aspect of the profession.

To the casual outside observer this will be unexpected and possibly even slightly bizarre news. Aren't veterinarians generally well respected? Isn't it a secure, interesting and rewarding career? Isn't it a dream job for so many people? Isn't it wonderful to heal innocent animals and get paid to play with fluffy kittens? All of that is true. Except the part about the fluffy kittens. Why, then, does darkness overwhelm so many of my colleagues? There are three significant reasons.

The first reason is that veterinary medicine attracts a disproportionate number of idealistic, introspective and sensitive people. Sensitive to the point of neurosis. This is true of all of the health professions, but it is even more so in veterinary medicine. Some of these introspective people are more comfortable around animals than around other people. They do not fully understand that it is actually a people job that happens to involve animals rather than the other way around. Grappling with this reality can be very problematic for some. Add to this the fact that competition to get into veterinary college is extremely high, and success favours perfectionists who can produce high marks. Perfectionism and idealism are fated to be brutally ground down by the chaos of reality in practice. And then their innate sensitivity lays them wide open to the second reason: the inherent and often surprising multi-factorial stress of the job.

Of immediate relevance to sensitive people is the fact that a veterinarian is at times marinated in death and grief. There are weeks — many weeks in fact — where I perform one or more euthanasias each day. Sobbing, crying, wailing, grief-stricken people, some of whom we've known for many years, are a routine part of our day. And for those of you who think this is simply a question of overwrought crazy cat ladies or frou-frou poodle people who too much resemble their dogs, I have two things to say to you. The first is that if you have not experienced a deep bond with an animal, then you are missing out on a key human experience, one shared by people from all walks of life, all backgrounds, all levels of intellect. It is one of the richest threads we weave. The second is that you have no more right to judge the grief of someone closely bonded to their pet than a blind man has to judge a photography exhibit. Simply trust me that these are normal people with legitimate and intensely felt grief. Additionally, a veterinarian is expected to be competent across a range of species and a range of disciplines, from dentistry to radiology to dermatology to . . . you name it, wedging the door wide open to so many opportunities to fail. And remember: "sensitive." Mix sensitivity and failure and see what happens. And I haven't even mentioned the financial stress of trying to be affordable to clients yet still able to service sometimes enormous debt burdens and meet payroll, etc. Or the stress of being a manager when you went to school to be a vet, not a manager. Or the angry clients. Or the angry spouse, upset because you're stuck late again.

The third reason is that we know how easy it is. How easy it is to die. Those daily euthanasias are consistently peaceful, painless, quick and reliable. One hundred percent reliable. We know the dose. We know the delivery methods. We have the drug right there. Can you see now why it happens too much?

And to make things worse, this is clearly an iceberg situation, where the suicides are only the visible tip of a massive mental health problem in the profession. According to an exhaustive American Veterinary Medical Association survey, just under a third of all veterinarians have experienced depression at least once since graduation. A smaller Canadian study found that one in ten veterinarians were *currently* classified as having depression, and another 15% were borderline. Also, a third of veterinarians in that study were suffering from anxiety, and a shocking 47% scored high on measures of emotional exhaustion. Clearly the problems run deep and run wide.

Fortunately, our professional associations are beginning to take notice, and mental health support is increasingly being incorporated into the services they provide. And what can you, the reader, do? You can't do much about the first and third reasons listed above, but you can definitely do something about the second. If your friend or family member is a veterinarian, do not trivialize their stress. Understand that the real job is far more complex and serious than you imagine. Offer to listen with an open heart. And if you are a client and your veterinarian has done something to make you angry, please recognize their human fallibility and frailty, and try to find a calm and respectful way to address your concerns.

And what about me? Well, fortunately I had a "happy optimist" chip deeply implanted at birth. The zombie apocalypse could roll into town and I would say, "Cool, this will make for some excellent photos!" And, "Maybe brains are better with a bit of smoked paprika?" I have painted a bleak picture when in fact most veterinarians are fine — even better than fine — but burnout is very real, and depression is very real, and, for a small, tragic minority, suicide is very real too. Not only in veterinary medicine, but in society at large, we must work to demolish the stigma that still surrounds mental health. If your leg is broken, everyone wants to talk about it, but if your brain is broken, hardly anyone does. This is wrong, and it is doing so much harm.

## CHOMP, CHOMP

Many people assume that veterinarians get bitten a lot. In fact, quite a few people seem to assume that this is the worst part of the job (not having considered the truly bad parts of the job I mentioned in the previous essay). I often get comments, accompanied by a wry chuckle, along the lines of, "It's a good thing you're seeing Killer today, Precious would take your arm off!" (Incidentally, this also illustrates a general principle that there is often an inverse correlation between the name of the patient and its behaviour.) I'll sometimes catch people mentally counting my ten intact fingers. The truth is that I've only been badly bitten twice. I've been in practice 28 years and see somewhere in the neighbourhood of a couple thousand patients a year. These are much better odds than you probably guessed.

That being said, the exceptions form an indelible mental rogues' gallery. Every veterinarian has one of these. At the top of mine is Oscar Westenheimer. Oscar was a little chihuahua cross (of course he was) who resembled a baked potato with four toothpicks stuck in for legs and an angry walnut for a head. Oscar was in for a nail trim. We knew that he had anger issues, so we were careful to muzzle him. The nail trim was done up on a table, and afterwards Oscar was set back on the floor, and then the muzzle was taken off. Have you guys been to Sea World? Or at least seen a video clip of when the trainer stands on a high platform and holds a fish out for Shamu, who then leaps cleanly out of the water to get the fish? Well, Oscar was Shamu, I was the inadvertent trainer, and my right index finger was the fish. How that little baked potato could catch so much air astonishes me to this day, but as soon as the muzzle was off, up he came. Sailing through the air, fangs sharpened, and then chomp, right through the fingernail. Off it came. This hurt. Fortunately the client wasn't there, so I was able to verbally express myself in a vigorous, honest and uncensored fashion.

The second time was more surprising. Despite the name (see first paragraph) I generally trusted Peaches, so I thought nothing of examining her mouth. I carefully opened her mouth, holding the upper jaw steady with my left hand while gently levering the lower jaw down with that poor right index finger. Chomp. I still don't know why she did this. Perhaps she had always wondered what it would be like to bite me? Perhaps she was hungry, and I didn't wash the sandwich residue off my hands thoroughly after lunch? Or maybe just early onset doggie dementia?

The reason we get bitten so (relatively) rarely is that the great majority of dogs will warn us using body language. I was probably too intent on chatting with the owner and on Peaches' tartar to tune in to her warnings.

Occasionally, though, you will encounter a sociopathic dog. A dog who does not conform to the norms of dog communication. A dog who is going to bite you just for the heck of it. So although it was not a "bad bite" (i.e., no wound dressings or antibiotics required), Daffodil deserves honourable mention in my rogues' gallery. She was a Brazilian German shepherd. Very expensive, very fancy. She sat perfectly beside her owner in the waiting room just as a very expensive, very fancy dog is expected to. The owner and I were talking, and I was leaning on the reception counter, perhaps as far away from them as the distance across the average living room. Daffodil looked very relaxed and at ease. And then, before I could flinch or even blink, she was across the room with her jaw clamped on my thigh. Half a second later she was back beside the owner, sitting primly again, as if nothing had happened. The owner seemed unfazed. I, however, was thoroughly fazed and excused myself to go take my pants off in the washroom. Daffodil hadn't broken the skin, but she had given me a temporary red dental chart tattoo.

What about cats? I've been lucky. Cats also generally give plenty of warning. A cat that is going to bite you radiates tension like a force field. I've also become very adept at carrying them gingerly like unexploded ordnance and handing them over to my staff, who are almost magical in their ability to manage the exploding cat. Usually. I do get scratched with tiresome regularity, though. Once the nails went right through my lab coat and my shirt, raking me across the chest and giving me a faintly piratical scar that I bear to this day.

But Oscar, oh Oscar: when I am one hundred years old and drooling and cannot remember that shoes go on my feet and not on my hands — I will remember you.

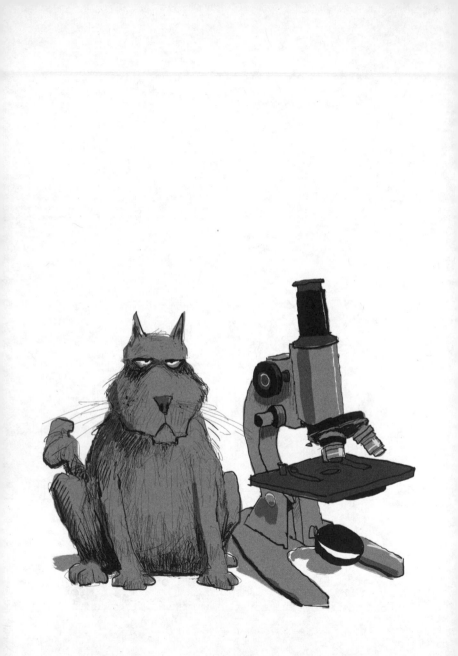

# PART 3

# THE SCIENCE OF VETERINARY MEDICINE

❖ ❖ ❖

## THE KNOWN UNKNOWN UNKNOWNS

I solemnly pledge that this will not only be the first time, but also the last time, that I will make reference to Donald Rumsfeld. In 2002 the then US Secretary of Defense famously said, "There are known knowns. There are things we know that we know. There are known unknowns. That is to say, there are things that we now know we don't know. But there are also unknown unknowns. There are things we do not know we don't know."

Veterinary practice is defined by the known knowns and known unknowns. But the unknown unknowns, such as the unknown pets with unknown diseases, are important too. Because we know that they must exist, they are actually the known unknown unknowns, if you follow me. You can, however, safely read on if you don't. There are no reliable statistics as to how many of these pets are out there, but in 2009 the Canadian Veterinary Medical Association published a survey showing that almost a quarter of dogs and half of cats owned by the respondents had not been to a veterinarian in the preceding 12 months. Keep in mind that people who participate in surveys tend to give answers that they think are more socially acceptable, so the real numbers are probably higher. Unfortunately, the survey did not dig deeper to determine how long it had been since those dogs and cats had seen a vet. Two years? Five years? Ever?

Why does this happen? Why do people fail to take their pet to the vet? Studies have looked at this too, and while the percentages vary, the main factors are as follows:

They don't see the point because the pet looks healthy to them.

They don't see the value in vaccination or other preventative measures.

They worry that it is going to be too expensive.

They worry that it is too stressful for their pet.

They feel that they can sort out a lot of issues on their own with the help of the internet.

Ah, the internet. You're probably expecting me to launch into a diatribe about the dangers of consulting with good old Dr. Google, DVM, but in fact there is a lot of helpful information out there. And a lot of harmful information too. And a lot of information that is outdated because it has just been cut and pasted from site to site over the years. Your veterinarian can help you sort out which information is valid, and which is not. I like to send people to VeterinaryPartner.com, and there are other similar sites as well that your veterinarian might recommend. But even the best information, regardless of the source, cannot replace experience and judgment and hands-on assessment. This should be obvious, but evidently it is not always.

If you're reading this, you're probably a reasonably regular visitor to your local vet clinic, so I imagine that I am, as the saying goes, preaching to the choir. Nonetheless, it bears stating clearly why regular veterinary visits are important. To begin with, animals age at anywhere from five to seven times the rate of humans, so our recommendation of annual visits is like saying you should go to your own doctor roughly a couple times a decade. Or to put it another way, the average healthy pet might see us a dozen to 15 times in their life. Hardly too often.

The next point is a blindingly obvious one. Animals don't talk. Veterinarians are not necessarily better at interpreting barks and meows, but we are trained to look for subtle clues regarding the animal's health. Often in life it is difficult to pick up on gradual changes in the familiar. Most parents have experienced the phenomenon of suddenly noticing how their child has grown when in fact it was of course happening every day, just a little bit. Animals instinctively hide signs of illness more so than humans, so without attention to these small chronic changes, something can be missed that might have been easier to treat before it became obvious.

Thirdly, there is a less obvious factor: building a relationship with a clinic and its veterinarians. If we know your pet and have seen it regularly, it makes it so much easier to quickly arrive at a competent response to a crisis. And a crisis will likely happen someday. How many people manage to get through their own lives without at least one urgent medical visit? Also, I would like to say that we treat absolutely everyone equally, and I know most of us really strive to, but we are human, and given the sometimes extreme demands on our time and attention, we will focus more on the pets we know than on the ones we don't. And we are more likely to do special favours, whether it's regarding the bill, or a possible house call, or an extra phone call, or more research, when we know the people and the pet. It's just the way it is.

All of the above is just in reference to check-ups. I haven't even mentioned the importance of regular preventative medicine, whether it be vaccines or treatments to prevent fleas or ticks or heartworm. These are all topics that I will explore in more depth in this section on the science of veterinary medicine. I will also share some stories on other (sometimes vaguely) scientific and medical subjects as an alternative to that charming but capricious Dr. Google, DVM, but of course never as a replacement for conversation with your own veterinarian. And if I can ask a favour of you: if you know somebody who has an "unknown unknown" pet, and you are done with this book, please pass it along to them.

Maybe they will learn something about veterinarians and veterinary medicine that will surprise them. And maybe, just maybe, this will lead to their pet becoming a happier and healthier "known known."

## THE PURR

Let's start our discussion of science with a cat story. A little one about one of this mysterious species' most asked-about mysteries: the purr.

Few things gladden the heart of a veterinarian like a healthy kitten check-up, especially if it is after a long series of messy, complex, sad, smelly or chaotic appointments (in other words, a normal day). You walk into the room, introduce yourself and then proceed to stroke a fluffy, happy kitten while discussing various easy kitten care subjects with the happy owners. I imagine that when some of you picture the life of the small animal veterinarian, you picture something like this. Well, it represents somewhere between 2 and 3% of what we do (see reference to sad, messy, complex, etc. above), but it is a lovely 2 to 3%. After the stroking and chatting you begin to examine said kitten. This is also pleasant as it hasn't learned to hate you yet. Then you place the stethoscope on the kitten's chest and hear . . . amplified purring. This may sound cute, but it is annoying as you really do want to hear the heart and lungs. There are a few different tricks to get them to stop, but my favourite is to carry the kitten with the stethoscope still in place over to the sink and then turn on the tap (slowly and carefully lest you freak the kitten out and the visit shifts into the messy, complex, chaotic column). This almost always surprises them enough to make them stop purring for a few seconds.

The owners typically chuckle about this and then sometimes ask, "So why do they purr?"

My answer: "We don't know."

I was tempted to end the story there, just for dramatic effect, but that would be irritatingly glib. And also disingenuous because although we don't know for sure, we do have some decent guesses now.

First of all, what actually *is* a purr? There used to be all kinds of wacky theories, but the answer ends up being the most obvious one: the purr comes from a vibration in the larynx (voice box) controlled by the rhythmic pulses of a neural oscillator in the brain. OK, the neural oscillator part may not be that obvious, but you might have guessed at the voice box. Cats with laryngeal paralysis can't purr. Some of you may have a cat that doesn't seem to purr. This does not mean that they have laryngeal paralysis, which is quite rare; rather, the thinking is that some purr so quietly that you cannot hear it. These cats will still have a vibrating larynx, but you would have to know exactly where to feel, how to feel and, most importantly, when to feel in order to detect this. The number who truly never purr is likely really very small, like people who truly never smile.

Which brings me to the main question, the why. Is it like smiling? The answer that is emerging from the fray of competing theories is that purring does resemble smiling in that it is used for social bonding, especially between kittens and their mothers (and cats and their owners with can openers). Moreover, like smiling, it results in endorphins being released. This also explains why cats don't just purr when they're happy, but also when they are injured or in pain. The endorphins provide natural internal pain relief. (Does this mean you should smile when someone punches you in the gut? Of course it does.) Even cooler, to my mind, is the well-supported suggestion that the vibrations from the 25–50 Hz frequency range of a cat's purr actually encourage tissue healing. The time may not be far off when we are told to strap a cat to our knee when we tear a ligament. Obviously some practicalities would have to be worked out first.

So is there any downside to purring? Potentially, yes. Search for "Smokey — The loudest cat in the world, 80 dB" on YouTube.

# THE WILD ARCTIC CHIHUAHUA

Mr. Jackson came in the other day with Bruiser, a 120-pound mound of muscle and fur who eats squirrels for lunch and begs to go outside when it's −40°C. Mr. Jackson was perplexed because Bruiser's DNA breed test had marked him as having rather a lot of chihuahua in him. Bruiser resembles a chihuahua the same way Mike Tyson resembles me.

By far and away the two most common questions I am asked by new puppy owners are "How big will he get?" and "What breed is he?" These are not subjects we are taught in veterinary school, and although with experience our educated guesses improve, they are still just educated guesses. The frustrating part is that some clients judge our overall skill and knowledge as veterinarians based on these guesses, and it can take years to live down a bad one. Consequently, I've honed the art of being vague while sounding knowledgeable.

The question of breed guessing was coincidentally on my mind that day as my own DNA test results had just come in. My wife had given me a 23andMe analysis as a gift, and one of the findings was that I am 3.2% Neanderthal, which puts me in the 99th percentile of all people tested. I like to think that nobody would have guessed this, but my wife disagrees.

Mr. Jackson had used a similar test that is available online for dogs (they mail you a cheek swab). He was not the first. I have had numerous clients over the years test their mixed-breed dogs, perhaps frustrated by my knowledgeable vagueness.

The most popular of these tests purports to identify a truly astonishing range of breeds, from Affenpinscher to Yorkshire terrier, including such oddities as Bergamasco, Glen of Imaal terrier and Xoloitzcuintli. I cannot vouch for the accuracy of this apparent extreme specificity, and in fact, at the risk of hearing from someone's lawyer, I will confess to a tiny bit of skepticism. In contrast, 23andMe is only willing to express confidence that I am generically "European," despite the fact that most of my known ancestors, back 13 generations in some cases, are specifically German. But getting back to dog breeds, I can say that despite the impressive list, the tests are missing one type of dog, and that gap trips people up here, and I suspect throughout western and northern Canada.

So here's the thing:

The thing is that many of our clients, including Mr. Jackson, get their dogs from shelters, and the shelters here are full of dogs from remote First Nations in the North. So, am I saying that the northern Manitoba bush is seething with packs of wild Arctic Chihuahuas? No. What I am saying is that when the Indigenous people came to North America across the Bering land bridge around 15,000 years ago, they brought dogs with them. These dogs were not any particular breed; they were simply, and quite beautifully, I might add, "dogs." The Aztecs began breeding these dogs into a specific line that became what we now know as chihuahuas. The DNA test then sometimes picks this up as the closest match for Bruiser and his friends. Look carefully at the next chihuahua you see and take note of the curled tail. The other breeds with curled tails are all northern breeds in the family group sometimes called the spitz type. Other members of this group are chows and Akitas, and their DNA sometimes also cross-reacts with our reserve dogs.

Fortunately for Mr. Jackson's ego, Bruiser's test also highlighted husky and Lab. Chihuahuas are actually very tough, but they do have an image problem with some people. Especially people who name their dog Bruiser.

## THE NATURE OF NATURE

Nature is not your friend, or your pet's friend. It is not your enemy either, but it is not your friend. It is simply indifferent. Like that cool, funny, attractive, intelligent person you wish you could get to know better, but they're too busy being themselves.

I'm probably going to get some hate mail for this, so let me first reassure the reader that I actually do love nature, regardless of how it feels about me. I spend as much time in the wilderness as possible, I contribute to environmental causes, I make my own yogurt, I buy eggs from pasture-grazed chickens direct from the farmer, I can distinguish the two species of nuthatch at 50 paces and I have been known to wear Birkenstocks. With socks.

Unfortunately, however, for some people, including some pet owners, love of nature has become confused with believing that medications and foods labelled "natural" are better for their pet's health. There are two distinct problems with this belief.

The first, as I indicated above, is that nature is not your pet's friend. The most potent cancer-causing agent yet identified anywhere is aflatoxin, which is produced by a certain mould on peanuts, rice and a few other foods. Tiny amounts that are undetectable to the eye, nose or taste buds are enough to cause a problem. Aflatoxin is perfectly natural and has been around since we were still living in trees and grunting at each other. And it has cropped up in some small-batch dog foods with poor quality control. This is just one example. There are many, many more.

Another way to look at this is to consider the lifespan of wild animals living fully natural lives. Wolves, for example, generally average around seven years, not much more than half the lifespan of many domestic dogs. Middle-aged and older readers may wish to shield their eyes, but if nature is indifferent to our fate, it is supremely indifferent to the point of negligent about our fate once we are past reproductive age.

The second problem with seeking out products labelled "natural" for health purposes is that the term is unregulated and effectively meaningless. I have no particular affection for the giant pharmaceutical corporations and their profit-seeking distortions of science, but if you believe that a product that happens to have a smiling Peruvian on the label and uses a funky, earthy font is truly natural and, moreover, is somehow made by a non-profit collective that only has your pet's very best interest at heart, then you are naïve. Ditto for pet foods named Purple Antelope or Green Beaver or some other marketing department–driven bewilderment. The only difference is scale. It's almost all profit driven, and it's almost all designed to sell as much product as possible.

If you can gather it or grow it or raise it or hunt it yourself, and if you have solid research (statistics, not anecdotes, please!) to back up its safety and efficacy, by all means, go natural! But if you are buying it packaged, be wary, be skeptical. It's not necessarily bad, but it's certainly not necessarily good either.

Many people have the charming belief that something wouldn't be allowed to be sold if it wasn't safe and at least a little bit effective. The truth is that if it doesn't require a prescription, it is either very loosely regulated or not regulated at all. A giant firehose of over-the-counter nutraceuticals, supplements, herbal remedies and "natural" cures of all description is aimed at us, and nobody has the resources to test and double-check even a fraction of it.

And as I write this, nature is producing −43°C wind

chills out there. So please keep your pets in the unnatural confines of the house until the natural winds subside.

## THE STOIC AND THE CASSANDRA

"He's not in pain, Doc. I checked him all over. Felt everything and he didn't react. I don't know why he's walking like that. Maybe there's something stuck in his paw that I can't see?"

Jake had come in with a pronounced limp, and Mr. Hudson had done exactly what any concerned pet owner would do and tried to find the sore spot. Some variation of this scenario plays out every day in the average small animal practice, sometimes several times a day.

I knelt down and greeted Jake, a friendly collie/Lab/shepherd mix, and gave him a couple of his favourite liver treats. He wagged his tail and was going to try to lick my face, but I moved his head aside to begin my exam before he could. I don't mind the occasional dog "kiss," but I knew that Jake was also a notorious poop eater. I began to palpate and manipulate each limb from the toes to the top, starting with the apparently normal ones and finishing with his right hind leg, the one he was limping on. (Incidentally, everyone thinks there is something stuck in the paw, but that is very rarely the case unless you see the dog chewing at the paw.)

"Like I said, Doc, I already did that, and I couldn't find anything that hurt."

Jake didn't react for me either, but I did feel a subtle swelling in his right knee joint, and he had what we call a "positive drawer sign," in which the tibia (shin bone) is able to slide forward relative to the femur (thigh bone), a bit like a drawer opening slightly. This meant that Jake had torn his cranial cruciate ligament, called the anterior cruciate ligament, or ACL, in humans. So, isn't that painful? If so, why wasn't Jake reacting? Yes, it is painful, and Jake was not reacting because he is a stoic.

Not that many dogs or cats have human "ouch, that spot hurts" reactions to pain. Some do, but most don't. Most are either stoics or Cassandras. The stoics, like Jake, prefer not to show any sign of pain. This is in part because in nature, showing pain can make you an easy target. This is especially true of prey species such as rabbits, who are ultra-stoic, but it is also true of social predators such as dogs, who might be in danger of losing status. That said, there is tremendous variation among breeds and among individual dogs.

So if stoics won't let you identify the location of the injury because they won't show pain, what do Cassandras do? In their most extreme form, Cassandras scream if you take a small step in their general direction. If they do let you examine them, they will show what seems like pain (more screaming) even if you are only vaguely in the vicinity of the problem area. You might be able to generally localize the problem as front end versus back end — maybe — but that's not all that helpful.

As a sweeping generalization, dogs are more likely to be stoics, and cats are more likely to be Cassandras, but there is a lot of crossover.

What is the poor veterinarian to do with the patient that not only refuses to speak English, but is likely a stoic or a Cassandra? As Jake's story illustrates, we perform a specialized kind of physical exam where we feel for what might be swollen, out of place, loose and yes, in some cases, sore. Sometimes X-rays are needed. And sometimes even then, we have to make educated guesses. Thank goodness for education!

## PILLING THE CAT

For your amusement, I invite you to type "pilling the cat cartoon" into the image-finding feature of your search engine. Have you looked at a few? Lots of lavishly bandaged people, right? Ha ha ha, right? Yes, all very funny — unless you have actually tried to administer a pill to your cat and have sustained multiple lacerations in the effort. So, in the interest of public service, I'm going to offer you two different injury-free strategies for pilling the cat.

Strategy #1: Don't. Don't pill the cat. No, I'm not telling you to toss your veterinarian's prescription in the bin and hope that thoughts and prayers will cure the illness instead. Rather, I am telling you that there are alternatives. Sometimes. People often assume that liquid medication is the main alternative, but I don't actually recommend that in most cases. There are a few drugs on the market that are flavoured with cats in mind and that require only small volumes to be administered, and these may be realistic, but many others are disastrous. At least with a pill you know where you stand — either it's in or it's out. With liquid, if they spit some out, you don't know how much of the dose they got. And it's messy. And your cat will hate you even more because the flavours of liquids are often more intense.

No, instead I suggest you ask whether the recommended medication comes as a long-acting injection (this mostly applies to antibiotics), or whether it can be made into a flavoured chewable treat. Quite a few drugs can be reformulated as treats in a surprising range of flavours. Tuna and chicken are the most popular in our practice. There's also beef, liver, bacon, salmon and the curiously non-specific "seafood." These can then be crumbled into similarly flavoured soft food if the cat won't take them directly as treats. The main downside of flavoured chews is that they need to be made by a compounding pharmacist, so there can be an extra wait and some extra expense.

Some people have luck with a product called Pill Pockets, which are ultra-tasty soft treats with a hollow part you hide the pill in when your cat is not looking. Incidentally, just hiding a pill in food very rarely works for cats. Some can tell even when you're just thinking about putting a pill in there and will refuse to eat until you stop thinking about it. And even if hiding the pill works at first, they usually catch on fairly soon, so it's only really feasible to try for short courses of medication.

Another don't-pill-the-cat solution is transdermal gel. Some drugs can be made into a gel, again by a compounding pharmacist, which is then applied to the ear and absorbs through the skin that way. This would be ideal if it weren't for the fact that skin absorption varies somewhat between individuals, so more monitoring is often needed. Also, it only works for a few medications. Nonetheless, it's worth asking your veterinarian about this option, especially for chronic meds.

Strategy #2: If you have to pill your cat, or for some dark reason actually prefer to pill your cat, there is a trick to it. I'm right handed, so I'll put the cat up on a table on my left side, with my left elbow keeping him against my body. I will have the pill ready between the thumb and forefinger of my right hand. I will then hold the top of his head with my left hand and gently tilt his head up. Next, I will use the middle finger of my right hand to pry his mouth open by pushing it into the space behind his fang teeth. (Stop laughing, I'm being serious.) As soon as he opens his mouth, you need to put the pill as far back over his tongue as you can and then immediately close the mouth. You should have a syringe or eyedropper ready with two or three millilitres of water. Squirt that in quickly by pushing it into the corner of his mouth, into his cheek. Blowing on the nose sometimes encourages him to swallow. And sometimes it encourages him to swat you. But the water is important, not only to make him swallow, but also because pills can otherwise sometimes become lodged partway down the esophagus (food tube), which can lead to serious complications.

Incidentally, as you are probably aware, most dogs are totally different. An article entitled "Pilling the Dog" would be exactly four words long: "Wiener. Cheese. Peanut Butter."

## THE FIREHOSE AND THE PUDDING

Most people are looking at this title and thinking to themselves, "That's weird. Firehose? Pudding? How do these relate to each other, or to pets or veterinarians? And he used the word 'firehose' in a previous essay. Is it about that?"

On the other hand, people who work in vet clinics are groaning lightly and face-palming because they know exactly what I am going to write about. I am going to write about diarrhea. And I'm going to try hard not to be too gross about it. It's tough for me, but I am going to try hard.

Even though it may seem obvious, let's start with a definition. From a medical perspective, diarrhea is stool that has enough liquid in it that it can no longer keep its happy log shape. A single abnormal bowel movement could be a fluke, but if it happens more than a couple times in a row, we can properly call it diarrhea. And if you want to get all nerdy and technical about it, you can refer to the Bristol Stool Scale and score the poops from one to seven. (If you have taken a moment to look at it online — you keener, you — please note that where it says "lacking fibre" for stools scoring five, this just applies to humans. In animals, I would consider five to be borderline diarrhea.) Poop that scores six is what we sometimes refer to as "pudding," and seven, if it is sprayed out, is "firehose." That's it for the gross bits! All done. You can read on safely now.

Once you know your pet has diarrhea, there are really just two important questions you need to consider: First, how long has it been going on? And second, does your pet have any other symptoms, or is she otherwise happy and normal?

To the first question, we're only going to talk here about diarrhea that has been going on less than roughly two weeks. This is acute diarrhea. The word acute sometimes confuses people as some believe it means severe, but it doesn't; it just means recent onset. Chronic diarrhea is due to a whole other set of causes, needs different tests and has different treatments. Fortunately, it is relatively rare. Acute diarrhea, on the other hand, is extremely common.

If the only symptom is diarrhea and there is no vomiting, lack of appetite or lethargy, then you can follow the advice here or just phone or email your veterinarian for their advice. There is no need to rush Billy Bob down for an urgent examination. If, however, any other symptoms are present, then it's best to get him checked over.

Before we get to what to do, a word about causes. Acute diarrhea in previously healthy pets with no other symptoms is almost always due to either a virus or what we like to call a dietary indiscretion. Even if your pet is not in contact with other animals, viral diarrhea is still possible as these viruses can be found out in the environment and be easily transmitted on their paws (dogs especially) or on your shoes. And dietary indiscretion simply means having eaten something their system doesn't tolerate, like five-day road-aged dead squirrel, stuffed pizza crust or a nasty random thing in the garbage (dogs especially, again). Keep in mind that what they can tolerate will change over time, so the fact that Ellie Mae did well on bacon chips for years doesn't mean that they won't cause diarrhea now.

Treatment for acute diarrhea is usually simple because the body has remarkable healing mechanisms. Often all we need to do is turn off the tap and power down the poop-making machine. To do this we need to temporarily replace their regular diet with a low-residue one that produces very little stool and therefore allows the gut to rest and heal. For this you have two options. You can either buy a commercial-prescription low-residue diet, such as Gastro or I/D, from your veterinarian, or you can cook for your pet. For dogs, the magic recipe is: one part extra-lean cooked ground beef (boil or fry and drain until it's just dry meat with no fat) — or, if your dog can't have beef, use lean chicken breast — and two parts (by volume, just eyeballing it is fine) boiled white rice (not brown).

That's it! Frequent small meals are best. And no treats or anything else other than water to pass their lips. For cats, I usually recommend just a pure lean protein source without the rice, such as canned fish packed in water, or cooked chicken or turkey breast.

Feed this until you've had 48 hours without diarrhea. If it still persists after that, please call your veterinarian! There may be no stool at all during this period, but this doesn't mean constipation; it is just the result of the low-residue diet producing very little waste. Once you're past the two days, mix the low-residue diet 50/50 with their regular food for a day or two before switching back completely.

One final wrinkle is that diarrhea that has been going on for a few days, but is not yet chronic, may be persisting due to dysbiosis, which is both a fun word to say and a useful one to know as it describes an imbalance in the normal gut bacteria. We are learning more and more how helpful the bacteria in the large intestine are. That dead squirrel or sidewalk virus can sometimes lead to a change in that bacterial population that impairs the gut's ability to produce normal stools. Consequently, if a couple days of low-residue diet haven't done the trick, your veterinarian may recommend a source of prebiotic, which is something that feeds healthy bacteria, such as canned pumpkin (weird but true), and/or a probiotic, which provides large numbers of the good bacteria. Years ago, we used to recommend yogurt for this, but fortunately there are much better, more dog and cat–specific probiotics available now from your veterinarian.

With any luck, ta-da, normal poop! (Ahem, Bristol Stool Scale three or four.)

## RAINBOW OF POO

Easily offended readers, or those with good taste, have probably not made it past the title to get to this warning, but as a precaution, here is the warning anyway: this piece is entirely devoted to discussing the whys and wherefores of dog poop colour. Yes, poop again. It's really important. That human medicine does not focus on it more astonishes me.

As I did not have a dog growing up, my earliest dog memories are of my friends' and relatives' dogs. In particular, I remember Antje, the beautiful, big black standard poodle owned by my friend Derwin Rovers's family. Derwin lived on the next block, and we were back and forth at each other's houses a lot. The Rovers were Dutch and loved the Dutch-style red cabbage that is stewed with apples and turns a vibrant purple colour. Derwin's Oma was visiting from the Netherlands, and she loved Antje. Antje loved her too. Antje loved her because Oma would feed her from the table whenever Derwin's parents weren't looking. One day they had this red cabbage, and Oma gave Antje rather a lot of it, plus some pork and mashed potatoes. The diarrhea was purple. Right on their white shag carpet. (This was the early 1970s, after all.) Brilliant, vivid purple. I cannot begin to explain how deeply impressive this was to a pair of six-year-old boys. Eyes wide, mouths hanging open, fingers pointing . . . this made our day. Heck, it made our month. Purple poo! Derwin, your dog had purple poo!

Fast forward 47 years, and I am still grappling with dog poo colour as not a week goes by without a question from a client about what it all means. So here, for your edification, is a field guide to the spectrum:

Brown: Let's start with an easy one. Any shade of brown is normal. It may vary from dark to light from time to time for no particular reason, but it's all good.

Yellow, Green or Orange: These are generally muted brownish versions of these colours, but these are also fine. You are just seeing more bile coming through. This may happen when the gut is contracting a little faster or with certain foods, but as long as it is firm, it is fine.

Red: This generates the most calls and visits as it is understandably alarming. Yes, red does mean blood. Generally, however, the red blood is in spots or streaks or as a small amount at the end of the bowel movement and should not be a cause for alarm. (If, on the other hand, the entire bowel movement is red, you are right to be alarmed, and you should call your veterinarian forthwith.) The spots and streaks just mean that the anus, rectum or last part of the colon are irritated, and that perhaps there was some straining that broke a small blood vessel. If it only happens once or twice, and the feces are otherwise OK or just a little soft, don't worry. If it happens several times, call your veterinarian.

Purple: See Antje's story above.

Blue: Never seen that. I have no idea. Call your veterinarian immediately.

White or Grey: Likely your dog was given a barium swallow test, and you are seeing the barium pass through. If this was not the case, you know what I'm going to say: call your veterinarian!

Black: This is the important one, really the only colour you need to watch for. If the stool is jet black like tar or molasses, and especially if it is soft and glistening and sticky, your dog *may* have what is called "melena" — that is, digested blood is coming from higher up in the system like the stomach or small intestine. This can be very serious as it may indicate a bleeding ulcer or tumour. Please note, however, that Pepto-Bismol can also turn the stool black.

So there you have it. While consistency, size, frequency and effort to produce are all important pieces of information regarding your dog's stool, colour, perhaps surprisingly, is generally not. Unless the colour in question is black.

And for the cat people reading, I'll say that more or less the same applies, although for some reason you don't ask about it nearly as often as dog people do. A fun fact though is that if you have multiple cats and someone is pooping out of the box, but you don't know who, you can put non-toxic sparkles in one cat's food at a time until you see whose sparkly poo is out of the box!

No, I have not lost my mind. Yes, I am absolutely serious about all of this.

❧ ❧ ❧

## BEGINS WITH THE LETTER "A"

Yes, gentle readers, today we are going to talk about your pet's anus. Frightened yet? If so, it's not too late to bail out and check if anything new has happened on Facebook in the last 15 seconds. But if you're still with me, you're in for a special treat, because we are not just going to be talking about the anus generally. Nope, we're going to be talking specifically about anal sacs.

Most people call them anal glands, but technically they are not glands, so veterinarians are taught to refer to them by their correct name: anal sacs. However, most veterinarians soon encounter the situation I did after just a couple years in practice.

"The problem is with Bella's anal sacs," I said.

The client raised her eyebrows and said with a smile, "You have to be very careful how you pronounce that."

Indeed. Naïvely, I hadn't considered this before. I don't often blush, but this was a flaming exception. Not long after that a colleague told me that he had decided to start an explanation of why there was inflammation around a dog's hind end by first describing the basic anatomy: "So, your dog has anal sacs . . ."

Outraged, the client interrupted, "He most certainly does not!"

So be very careful how you enunciate that third"a." Or just call them anal glands.

And why do they have these bizarre little structures, you ask? They have them primarily to use for scent marking. All carnivores have them. Skunks have the most famous anal sacs, having turned a communication device into a weapon. But for our dogs and cats, the stinky secretions contain information about them. What information, specifically, we don't know, but we can guess gender and perhaps some individual identification markers. This is why dogs in particular will sniff poop. They are not necessarily interested in the poop itself, but rather in the bit of anal sac material that is on it.

This then leads to the question of how these sacs normally empty. They empty when the animal has an appropriately sized bowel movement. The pressure as it passes through the anus squeezes the anal sacs. When this does not happen, perhaps because there has been diarrhea or unusually small stools, or just at random in some individuals, then the material can gradually build up and lead to problems. Typically, a dog or cat with full sacs will lick at the area or begin to "scoot" in an unmistakable fashion whereby they sit down and then drag their bottom across the ground by pulling themselves along with their front legs. Note: scooting is not caused by worms! This old myth is remarkably persistent.

If they are successful in emptying their sacs by scooting or licking, you will know — the smell is memorable. Gram for gram, anal sac secretion is one of the most potently vile substances on the planet. However, if they are unsuccessful, you should call your veterinarian. One of the more glamorous parts of our job is to put on a latex glove, apply a little lubricant and manually express full anal sacs. And here's the cool part — if your dog has frequent issues with full anal sacs, we can teach you how to express them at home!* No medical degree required! It's clearly not for everyone, though.

If the sacs remain too full for too long, the material can thicken and become difficult to express. This thickened material can also become infected, leading to the formation of an anal sac abscess. Some dogs do not give clear warning signs like scooting, so unfortunately the first thing you may notice is blood near the anus when the abscess ruptures. Luckily this is usually easily treated with antibiotics, but it can be an alarming mess in the meantime.

Prevention is of course always better than treatment. There is no foolproof way to prevent anal sacs from filling up, but adding fibre to the diet can help. A source of fibre, such as Metamucil, oat bran or canned pumpkin,

---

* For the inexplicably curious, the For Dummies series actually has an online tutorial on this.

can increase the bulk of the stools and thus encourage the sacs to empty naturally. Appropriate amounts vary with the source of fibre and the size of your dog, so check with your veterinarian. Incidentally, we generally do not add fibre to a cat's diet, but cats are fortunately much less likely to have issues with their anal sacs. One final note is that in some animals, food allergies may play a role in anal sac disease, so ask your vet about that possibility.

I got through that without even telling my grossest anal sac story! I'm proud of myself.

## YELLOW

After writing "Rainbow of Poo," it was only a matter of time before I turned my attention to the colour of pee. It should be obvious that I will not be talking about rainbows here.

Pee is yellow. This much you know. But why is it yellow? Do you know? Do you even care? Quickly then, a bit of science (cue the booming voice echoing "science, science, science" like in an '80s educational show). Urine is yellow because of the presence of urobilin. Urobilin is a breakdown product of bilirubin, which also gives bile its yellowish colour. And bilirubin is in turn a breakdown product of hemoglobin. As red blood cells are constantly being turned over (in the average human, 100 million red cells die each day, but fortunately 100 million are born each day as well), there is a constant stream of urobilin waste the body needs to get rid of.

Urine is full of all sorts of other waste products as well, most notably urea, which is a by-product of protein metabolism. These other waste products are colourless, though, and the urobilin is excreted at a more or less constant rate, so the only variable in how yellow the pee is is how much water is being excreted. More water means more dilute urobilin and less yellow, and less water means more concentrated urobilin and more yellow. Logical, yes?

So now that you know this, what can you do with this information? The first thing to understand is that urine concentration will vary from day to day, so one really clear pee or one really dark yellow pee doesn't mean much. If, however, your dog (I'll get to cats later) is producing very clear pee day after day, there may be something wrong. There may be. It may also be that he just loves to drink water and his body is getting rid of the excess. But definitely get it checked out to rule out diabetes, kidney disease, adrenal gland disease, etc. If your dog is producing very dark yellow pee day after day, he may be dehydrated, and you should call your veterinarian to discuss.

That's all well and good for dogs, but what about cats? You'll only see the colour of your cat's pee if you are invading their privacy much too closely, or if you are unlucky enough to have the pee appear on a white towel or bedsheet. However, if you use clumping litter, you can use the size of the clumps as a way to guess at concentration, because as volume goes up, concentration tends to go down, and vice versa. If the clumps start getting much larger, the urine is possibly becoming more dilute and you should contact your veterinarian. By the same token, if the clumps are getting smaller, make sure dehydration is not an issue.

What about other colours? Red is the only one worth talking about. Any redness or pinkness in the urine could indicate a problem such as an infection or inflammation or stones and needs to be brought to your veterinarian's attention. Also, if it is April 1, collect a normal sample, put some blue food colouring in it and drop it off at your clinic.

Finally, a few random facts about pee:

Many people assume that a pet in kidney failure will stop producing urine. The opposite is in fact true. Up until very close to the end, kidney failure patients produce a lot of dilute urine. The kidneys are failing to concentrate the urine, not failing to make it.

Urine kills grass because the urea being excreted is high in nitrogen. It's like dumping a bunch of nitrogen fertilizer in one spot.

Stinkier dog pee usually just means more concentrated pee (unless you've fed your dog asparagus or something strange). I actually get this question a lot. Infection is a possible cause too, but generally there are other symptoms, such as accidents, urgency or straining.

Dogs and cats can tell large numbers of other specific dogs and cats apart by their urine scent, so all that sniffing your dog does on a walk is about figuring out who was there and whether they know them. A longer, deeper sniff usually means that it was an unfamiliar animal. It's a pretty darned exciting day for Orbit, my dog, when I come home from work after being peed on.

## BREAD AND EARS

Whack, whack, whack — the metronome of Timmy's tail kept striking the wall beside him, speeding up as I approached with the expected liver treat. You know how some dogs smile? Timmy definitely smiled. An ultra-wide, happy black Labrador retriever smile.

"He really loves those treats!" Mrs. Singh said.

"Timmy doesn't just love these treats," I thought, regarding his beer-keg-shaped torso. But he was a happy dog and a good patient, and we weren't going to discuss his weight again today. Today we were going to discuss his ears again.

"So, his ears are bugging him again?" I asked as I crouched down to scratch Timmy's neck and then carefully lift up his right ear flap. The tail metronome slowed down a little.

"Yes, he started shaking his head again yesterday, and I don't have any drops for him anymore."

Timmy's right ear was bright red, and the ear canal was filled with a sharp-smelling black substance. I gently inserted the tip of my otoscope to look a little deeper down the canal. The whack, whack, whack of Timmy's tail stopped entirely. He wasn't smiling anymore either, but he stayed still and let me perform the examination. When I was done I straightened up, gave Timmy another treat and told Mrs. Singh, "I'm afraid it's a yeast infection again."

Often I will swab the ear and look under the microscope to make sure that I know what is growing in there, but in this case it was so characteristic, and it had happened so many times before, that it wasn't necessary. Mrs. Singh was horrified the first time Timmy developed a yeast infection because she associated it with yeast infections in people, but it is a very different situation in dogs' ears.

Yeast are normally resident on their skin and in their ears in low numbers. We all have a beneficial ecosystem of bacteria and yeast living on us in balance with our system. The yeast are, however, similar to baker's yeast in that they will multiply rapidly in warm or moist conditions. If a dog's ear canal becomes inflamed, it is like turning the oven on when you're getting ready to bake bread. This is especially true for dogs with big ear flaps (closing the oven door!). Dogs with more erect ears do occasionally also get these sorts of infections, but they are much less common. As the yeast multiply, they create that strong, smelly, waxy discharge, and they further inflame the ear, creating a vicious circle of ever-worsening inflammation and yeast infection.

OK, you say, that makes sense — but why are the ears inflamed in the first place? In a word: allergies. While there are some other triggers, allergies account for the great majority of these inflammations. This sometimes surprises people because they were unaware that dogs could have allergies, and they are surprised that the allergies would only affect the ears. Regarding the first surprise, indeed dogs do have allergies. Do they ever! Allergies are in fact extremely common, especially in some breeds. There is a whole separate lengthy conversation that can be had about allergies, but for the purposes of the ear discussion, suffice it to say that they are usually environmental allergies to house dust, pollen or mould, and occasionally food-related allergies to the primary source of protein in the diet. Allergies can come on at any age and can change over a pet's life. And with respect to only affecting the ears, in part this is because the ears have the most sensitive skin in the body, and in part it is because the closed-oven-door feedback loop makes allergies there far more obvious. Incidentally, you'll recall that I mentioned that moist conditions can also encourage yeast to grow, so occasionally we will see these infections after a dog has been swimming or been bathed.

I had explained all this to Mrs. Singh before, but she found she just couldn't stick to a diet for Timmy to try to address a possible food allergy, and she wasn't that interested in going down the more complex path of pursuing environmental allergies. The drops worked well, and she preferred to just refill them as needed. I explained again the need to clean the ears regularly as the normal self-cleaning mechanism had been damaged by the repeated infections. And I explained again the need to finish the entire course of drops rather than stopping as soon as the symptoms subsided, but I could see that she was beginning to tune me out. I was refilling the drops, and that's what she'd come for. And you know what? To be honest, it's not like I follow each and every piece of advice my doctor or dentist gives me. Just ask me about flossing . . . Everyone just does their best. All we doctors can do is try to nudge the definition of "best" a little further along.

Now that the poke, poke, poke and the blah, blah, blah had stopped, the whack, whack, whack began in earnest again. Timmy knew we were done, and he was wagging and smiling and so clearly hoping for a goodbye liver treat that I had to smile right along with him.

## COUGH, HACK, WHEEZE

There are four exam rooms along the hall leading to my office. The other day when I arrived at work, two of the four had signs on their doors stating "No Dogs!!" No, this does not mean that we are transforming into a cat clinic (although there are moments during heartworm season when this starts to sound attractive). Instead it means that we are going through another outbreak of "kennel cough" and have to sanitize some rooms.

Kennel cough is an unfortunate name as it is misleading. Being a nerd, I prefer the far more accurate "infectious tracheobronchitis," but we nerds are an embattled and misunderstood minority. The main problem with the name kennel cough is the kennel part. Dogs can contract this disease any time they are in close contact with disease carriers, especially indoors, but not just in kennels. The easiest way to understand this disease is to think of it like the human common cold. Sure, schools and daycares (i.e., kennels for kids) are really easy places to pick up colds, but anywhere you are mixing with other people can do the trick. The cough part of the name is occasionally also misleading as some people perceive their dog to be choking or gagging or retching, rather than coughing. This can be even more confusing because a violent coughing fit can lead to hacking up some phlegm or saliva, which can easily look like vomiting to the anxious pet owner.

But all of that notwithstanding, I am not going to change the minds of thousands (ha!) with one essay, so for the sake of clarity, let's keep calling it kennel cough. Now I suppose I should explain what it is. I already tipped my hand above when I compared it to the human common cold. Humans with colds may sneeze more than cough because their nasal passages are targeted whereas dogs almost exclusively cough because it preferentially hits their windpipe and bronchi, but otherwise the analogy is useful in several ways.

Like the human cold, kennel cough

- Is very contagious, but not all individuals will be affected the same way as some have immunity.
- Is caused by a large number of different organisms. In humans, it's only viruses. In dogs, it's mostly viruses plus one bacterium (Bordetella) and something wacky that is neither virus nor bacteria, called a mycoplasma.
- Usually runs a course of one to two weeks and requires no medical intervention.
- Can occasionally develop secondary complications such as pneumonia or bacterial bronchitis, especially in the weak, the otherwise ill, the very young and the very old.

Consequently, if your dog is coughing but is still hoovering his food and racing around like the damn fool he is, please give your veterinarian a call before rushing down. We don't want to spread the bugs in the waiting room and can often triage and give useful advice over the phone. (Colleagues, please don't send me hate mail for suggesting this.) Sometimes we may recommend a cough suppressant if the cough is disrupting sleep or is otherwise distressing. However, we must see the ones that might have secondary complications. These dogs may be depressed, off their food and/or hacking up thick yellowish goo when they cough. In puppies, any vomiting, diarrhea or nasal discharge at the same time as the cough is also a reason to come down.

One distinction between kennel cough and human colds is that we have vaccines for kennel cough. These vaccines primarily protect against Bordetella and some also cover a couple of the viruses. Because of the number of potential causative organisms, these vaccines only help reduce the risk, they do not guarantee protection the way a rabies or distemper vaccine does. Nonetheless, risk reduction is still useful in high-risk scenarios such as, you guessed it, kennels, dog daycares and training classes. Many of these facilities require proof of vaccination because they want to reduce the chance that they'll have 20 dogs coughing simultaneously. The risk in off-leash dog parks is variable and usually quite a bit lower although it depends on how nose-to-nose your dog gets. Think of it like daycares versus playgrounds for kids. The daycare is a petri dish sitting in an incubator, but in the playground your child will only get more colds if they lick the slide or wrestle with their friends rather than swinging quietly alone.

## THAT DISTEMPERMENT SHOT

You don't have to be in practice very long before you have someone come in with an out of control puppy, expressing relief that the puppy is about to get his "distemperment" shot. "He's getting that distemperment shot today, right, Doc? I can't wait until he settles down!"

"Um . . . yeah . . ."

To be fair, it is an odd and confusing name. Its origins reach back to before the advent of modern medicine. Before the mid-19th century the prevailing theory was that good health resulted from a balance between the four "humours," also called "tempers": blood, yellow bile, black bile and phlegm. You can still see it in the language today — melancholy is Greek for black bile, and indeed depressed people were thought to suffer from an imbalance of the humours with an excess of black bile. (For the record, actual bile is a greenish yellow, but you probably already knew that.) Dogs stricken with distemper were so profoundly ill and could potentially spew phlegm, bile and blood (in the stool), so they were thought to be dis-tempered.

And what is distemper actually? It is a disease caused by a virus that is related to the human measles virus, although the symptoms are very different. Dogs with distemper often have a constellation of symptoms including fever, heavy nasal discharge, breathing difficulties, vomiting, diarrhea, blindness and eventually nervous system symptoms up to and including seizures in some cases. It is spread through the discharge from a sick dog. The incubation period is up to about five days between exposure and first symptoms. There is no specific treatment, only supportive care, which often has to be quite intensive to prevent the patient from succumbing. Even so, about half of infected dogs will die.

Confusingly, feline distemper, more correctly called panleukopenia, is not related to canine distemper. It is in fact a close cousin of canine parvovirus.

Incidentally though, canine distemper can also spread to wildlife. Foxes, coyotes and wolves are definitely susceptible, and a mutated form has spread to seals as well, where it has devastated some populations. Oddly some marsupials are also vulnerable, and distemper is theorized to have played a role in the extinction of the magnificent Tasmanian tiger (also called the thylacine).

That's all the bad news, but the good news is that the vaccines are extremely effective and safe. Consequently, distemper is now very rare in areas where vaccination is common, such as here in the city. When we do see cases, it is usually in puppies from remote communities. In the Arctic and in isolated First Nations, it is still rampant.

Actually, I lied. That wasn't all the bad news. There is a worrying trend among some pet owners to refuse vaccination. How often to booster is a subject of some legitimate debate, but not to vaccinate at all is foolhardy (to be polite). It is still a small minority of pet owners who refuse to vaccinate, and fortunately their pets are protected by the fact that the majority of their neighbours are more sensible and responsible, so the virus cannot yet gain a foothold, but this could change. On the human side, whooping cough outbreaks are beginning to become more frequent in areas where vaccination rates are dropping. Whooping cough is sometimes fatal in babies.

Distemper is far deadlier than whooping cough.

And training is the remedy for "distemperment." Now, if only we had a shot for that.

✿ ✿ ✿

## SPAY DAY

Assuming the Hudson's Bay Company's lawyers remain quiet, every November, the Manitoba Veterinary Medical Association will sponsor a "Spay Day." The event features significant discounts on spaying and neutering at participating clinics.

This is the perfect opportunity to explain what exactly spaying is and why we do it. Let's start with that weird word, "spay." It's made a long journey from the Latin "spatha," meaning broad sword (kind of alarming), from which we also get spade and spatula, to the Old French "espeer," meaning to cut with a blade, and then over to England, where it turns up as "spaier" and "spaied," which is where things get . . . weird. There it was first used to describe a specific way of dispatching a deer with a thin blade during the hunt, but in 1410 there also is reference to "oon spaied biche lesteth lengere in hure bounte than other ii that byn not spaied." How they managed to "spaied" the "biche" and have her survive in 1410 is unclear, but henceforth, the word was associated with the removal of ovaries from prized hunting dogs, from which the evolution to the modern usage is obvious.

I'm sorry, that's probably way more than you wanted to know about that, but I was on a roll. In any case, yes, it's a weird word.

The technical term is clearer though: ovariohysterectomy. How is that clear? Just break it down: "ovario" means ovaries, "hyster" means uterus (ok, that bit's not exactly clear) and "ectomy" means removal. In fact, this may be a useful thing to know. Any surgery ending in the suffix "ectomy" involves removing something. So when your own doctor starts saying "blahblahectomy," pay close attention. For the record, the suffix "otomy" means making a temporary hole somewhere, and "ostomy" means making a permanent or semi-permanent hole somewhere. Come to think of it, you should probably also tune in when the doctor says "blahblahostomy."

Now that I've squandered half the essay on terminology, let's move on to something useful: questions I have been asked about spaying.

1) The big one: I won't let my dog out to get pregnant, so why spay?

We have a saying: "all pets get spayed, it's just a question of whether it's an elective or an emergency procedure." This is because of something called pyometra. People will sometimes argue that they do not want to spay because it is "unnatural," forgetting that what nature intends is for the animal to become pregnant with every cycle. When this does not happen, and they unnaturally cycle "empty," there is a significant risk that the open cervix and waiting uterine bed will invite bacteria in, causing a life-threatening pyometra infection. According to one study, 23% of intact female dogs under the age of ten develop pyometra. The rate goes up quickly over the age of ten.

2) OK, got it, but why not just a hysterectomy?

To begin with, it's not any easier or quicker as the ovaries are right there by the uterus anyway, and while it would be just as effective in preventing pregnancy, leaving the ovaries behind would allow a dog to continue to have heat cycles. And why is this a problem? In dogs, this is a problem because 12–16% of dogs who have gone through a heat cycle will develop mammary (breast) cancer whereas almost no dogs who are spayed before the first heat develop it. Many of these are benign cancers, but they still require surgery — often many surgeries — and some are malignant. In cats it's even worse, as 90% of mammary tumours are malignant. Moreover, anyone who is thinking about leaving the ovaries in their cat has not spent any quality time in the company of a cat in heat.

3) Yeah, but what about the risks?

There is always some statistical level of risk with any surgery and general anaesthetic, but this is an extremely routine and safe procedure in veterinary medicine. In the 28 years I have been in practice, I cannot recall seeing a single death related to a spay. That's not to say that it can't happen, but the risk of death due to pyometra and mammary tumours is an order of magnitude higher.

4) But what about these longer-term knee joint risks I've been reading about?

Clever you. Nothing in life gets any simpler with time, does it? Everything becomes more complex. Yes, in the last few years more evidence has come to light linking early spaying in some breeds with an elevated risk of tearing the cruciate ligament in the knee. What is meant by early, and how much is the risk elevated? I'm going to be a wimp and tell you to ask your veterinarian. This really does have to be addressed case by case as a number of factors come into play.

So if you're in Manitoba, or somewhere else that celebrates Spay Day, find the date and mark it on your calendar. I suspect that most of you reading this have pets who are already spayed, so use that day to congratulate them on their spayedness.

# GETTING TUTORED

In a straw poll, veterinarians stated that their favourite *Far Side* cartoon was the one where a dog being driven to the vet brags to his friend, "I'm going to the vet's to get tutored!"

This is funny several ways, but the way that is relevant to this piece is that it highlights the confusion around the terminology of spaying and neutering. Even well-educated clients will approach the subject cautiously: "I guess it's time to get Fred . . . is it spayed, or neutered?"

For my lay readers, neuters are for males and spays are for females. At the risk of sounding unprofessional, a handy mnemonic is that the word "neuters" contains the word "nuts." Which brings me to the next area of confusion: the widespread misunderstanding of what this procedure actually entails.

So the technical term for neuter is actually orchidectomy. "So, Doc, you're taking out his . . . *orchids*???" Yeah, so that's why we don't use that term at all. A more descriptive term is castration. Large animal veterinarians routinely and happily call it that. The companion-animal world is different, however. Picture a sweet little old lady with her tiny, fluffy white poodle sitting neatly on her lap. He has a blue bow at the base of each ear and smells faintly of peaches. Now picture me saying, "Yes, Mrs. Butterworth, it's time to castrate Baby." Moreover, there are people who think that castration means cutting the penis off. Yikes! Yes, there are people who believe such things. And no, we never do that (except in very special circumstances in cats who have frequent urinary obstructions, but I digress).

What do we do then? We do this: we surgically remove the testicles. (Remember? "Neuters" contains "nuts"?) Sometimes I'm asked why we don't just perform a vasectomy instead. This is because reproductive control is only one of the reasons to neuter. In many cases, we would also like to remove the ability to produce testosterone in order to eliminate the risk of testicular cancers and chronic prostate infections later in life as well as to help curb marking behaviour, roaming and male-on-male aggression. You'll note that I wrote "help curb." Too often people use neutering as a substitute for training. It is not.

Now I'm going to wade into a controversial area. Virtually all pet cats are neutered. The exceptions involve people who have had their own olfactory nerves removed. However, not all dogs are neutered, at least not at the traditional six months of age, and — here is the controversial bit — this might be OK. As I touched on in the last essay, there is evidence now that breeds of dogs that are prone to cruciate knee ligament ruptures (typically large breeds) may be at increased risk if they are neutered before their bodies are fully mature. This might mean waiting until 18 or 24 months for some breeds. There may be other risks associated with early neutering in some dogs as well. This is a complex area of ongoing research, so please (please, please) speak to your veterinarian first before making any decisions based on what you have read here or on the internet. A lot of what we do has evolved from boiler-plate one-size-fits-all recommendations to a discussion of options tailored to the risk/benefit ratio specific to your pet. And this is a good thing. A confusing thing, but a good thing.

I guess that was more like toe-dipping than wading.

Finally, I'm going to leave you with one word: "neu-ticles." Fake testicles so that he can keep his manly appearance. Go ahead, google it. Yes, they are 100% for real. And endorsed, it seems, by Kim Kardashian. Finally, there is help for the owner who wants to neuter their dog but has an unhealthy personal attachment to the appear-ance of the dog's scrotum. Unfortunately, it's not the help these people actually need. Comes with a nifty bumper sticker though!

❧ ❧ ❧

## TAKE THE PARKA CHALLENGE

OK, now that summer is well and truly here, I would like to issue a challenge to dog owners. Those of you whose dogs have long fur or an undercoat, please put a parka on. Those of you with short-furred, single-coated dogs, a spring or fall jacket will do. And if your dog has hairy or floppy ears, pull up the hood or put on a toque. Got it? Now here's the fun part: leave it on 24 hours a day . . . forever. Anyone up for this? Waiting . . . Waiting . . . Come on, you guys!

To be fair, and to make this challenge realistic, you are permitted to grow a Gene Simmons tongue and to leave it hanging out constantly for cooling.

I think we sometimes forget that our ancestors evolved in the tropics. As a result, we have an amazing cooling system with our ability to both dilate the tiny blood vessels called capillaries and sweat just about anywhere on our (mostly) hairless bodies. Our dogs' ancestors evolved in the subarctic, which has consequently equipped them for cooling only with a big tongue that drools and a little nose that sweats (and sweaty paw pads, but that's useless). We've created a few more heat-tolerant breeds, such as Chihuahuas, that have much thinner, shorter coats and big, erect ears for some of that capillary dilation action, and there is the occasional goofball black Lab who likes to sprawl in the sun, but the majority of our dogs dislike the heat.

How do you know that your dog is hot? Simple: panting. I get a lot of questions about panting dogs as people sometimes worry that it is a sign of something serious. Very rarely it can be an indication of a fever or of heart or respiratory disease, but if there aren't any other symptoms of those problems, your dog is almost certainly panting for one of three reasons:

1. He's hot.
2. He's stressed, anxious or excited.
3. He's in pain.

You should rule out stress, anxiety, excitement and pain first, but chances are, your dog is simply trying to cool off. This does not necessarily mean that he is suffering, no more so than a person who is sweating is suffering, but it does mean that you should be aware that he is hot and might actually be too hot.

The solutions are hopefully too obvious to bother mentioning, but I'll do it anyway (in a handy numbered list again!):

1. Professional grooming.
2. Early morning and late evening walks.
3. Access to cool resting areas in the house.
4. Moving to the Arctic.

🐾 🐾 🐾

## THE CATS WHO MIGHT BE CANARIES

I pride myself on knowing stuff, so I hate it when I don't. And this occurs more often than I would normally care to admit. Consequently, when Abby Matheson, a woman who has owned many, many cats for many, many years asked me why there never used to be any hyperthyroidism, I was both stumped and annoyed with myself.

She was right. It was only in 1979 that reports began to emerge of a new disease in cats. Older cats were losing weight rapidly despite a good appetite. A veterinarian in New York figured out that these cats had developed benign tumours in their thyroid glands that caused the gland to produce excess thyroid hormone — a condition called hyperthyroidism. Soon, hyperthyroid cats were being diagnosed all around the world. By the late 1980s, when I was going to veterinary school, it was estimated that one in ten cats would develop it. Where did this disease come from? New diseases did occasionally arise, but they were always infectious diseases with clear origins, such as canine parvovirus, which was the mutation of the cat distemper virus, and heartworm, which was the northward migration of a tropical disease.

Some speculated that it was just that cats were living so much longer that we were now seeing more geriatric diseases, but this made no sense as the gains in life expectancy were gradual and the apparent emergence of hyperthyroidism was relatively sudden. Veterinarians, being neurotic as a group, also blamed themselves, assuming they had just missed it before. This also made no sense as the disease is dramatic and obvious in its advanced form. One researcher looked through 7,000 old autopsy reports and found no evidence of hyperthyroidism. It really was a new disease.

Various other more reasonable, but still flawed, hypotheses were put forward through the 1990s and 2000s, but to speed the story along, I'll take you straight to what appears to be the answer. In four letters, it is PBDE. This is the acronym for polybrominated diphenyl ether, a common fire-retardant found especially in furniture foam, carpet underlay, some clothing and bedding and in the plastic housing for some electronics. PBDEs gradually, microscopically, shed into the home environment and become part of the dust. Cats, being close to the ground, are exposed to dust even in relatively clean houses. And crucially, PBDEs have been shown to be endocrine disruptors, meaning that they can interfere with hormonal functions. Thyroid is a hormone. Tellingly, PBDEs first became widespread during the 1970s. This is all circumstantial evidence, but the research evidence is mounting as well with a steady stream of ever more persuasive studies.

PBDEs were declared toxic by the Canadian government in 2004, and their manufacture and import was restricted. Unfortunately though, they are still pervasive in the environment, and industry has side-stepped the regulations by devising new fire-retardant chemicals that may or may not have the same effects. Nobody knows yet. Government regulations are slow to play catch-up. Nonetheless, I think I am seeing fewer cases of hyperthyroidism than I did back in the '90s. What I am seeing far more of is pancreatitis. Canine pancreatitis is more or less unchanged, but feline pancreatitis has skyrocketed from a very rare diagnosis 20 years ago to a weekly one now. Did we just miss it before? The discussion is starting to sound familiar . . .

Everyone has heard the expression "canary in the coal

mine." Before the advent of modern toxic gas detectors, coal miners did actually bring canaries down into the mines. The birds were far more sensitive to the buildup of carbon monoxide than humans, so when they began showing signs of poisoning, it was an early warning for the miners to get out of there. In this context it may be interesting to note that the incidence of human thyroid cancer has increased more rapidly than most other cancers since the late 1970s. This is far from conclusive and studies are ongoing, but maybe our cats are telling us something. Maybe we should listen more carefully.

## THE C WORD

Yes, cats and dogs get cancer. And turtles, and goldfish, and budgies and rats. Actually, especially rats. As a very general rule, most diseases exist in some form in most animals. We are really all remarkably similar under the hood. Yet people are sometimes surprised to hear it. And of course, they are upset to hear it. It is the most feared diagnosis after all.

But there are some things you should know about cancer. First of all, it is not one disease, but rather a large family of diseases. Really whenever cells begin to divide in an uncontrolled fashion, it is technically cancer. Everything from that gross little warty thing on the top of Buffy's head right through to the aggressive volleyball-sized thing that caused Duke's liver to fail. When these dividing cells don't destroy important tissues or spread through the system, we call it benign cancer. When they do, we call it malignant cancer. Fortunately, most cancers are benign. To reduce confusion, a lot of us try to avoid calling the benign ones cancer at all and will refer to them as tumours or growths, but you should always ask if you are unclear — is it benign or malignant?

The second thing you should know is that even malignant cancer is not a death sentence. In human medicine many cancers are increasingly viewed as chronic diseases that, even if they cannot be cured, can be managed well enough to allow a good quality of life for a reasonable length of time. That is our goal in veterinary medicine too, with a strong overriding emphasis on the quality of life aspect. Ultimately it does not matter what label we put on the disease; what matters is what we can do to provide a good quality of life. The cancer label is not helpful — there are many non-cancer diseases that are worse than many cancers. To be sure, there are too many cancers where we have to move rapidly to a euthanasia conversation, but my point is to not view all cancers the same way as there are some that can be easily managed to provide that good quality of life for some time.

I am sometimes asked, "Aren't we just prolonging his life?" If I'm in the right mood, and if I know the client well, my answer to that is, "Every time you take a breath, you are prolonging your life!" It's true. The name of the game for every organism is life prolongation, just so long as it is without suffering. An animal doesn't know how long it's supposed to live. It has no thought for tomorrow and no anxiety when I tell their human companion that we can probably only keep it comfortable for another six weeks. Each happy day for an animal is a happy day. It's that simple. We just want to string together as many of those happy days as we can.

The other stumbling block in treating cancer in pets is the word "chemotherapy." Some people react quite strongly when I suggest it, as if I've now crossed a line into ridiculous territory. But chemotherapy just means drugs to treat cancer, and much like the cancers themselves, there is a huge amount of diversity in these drugs. The most common treatment for a malignant bladder cancer is the same drug we use for arthritis (a non-steroidal anti-inflammatory). Used for cancer, it is "chemotherapy" (oooh! aaah!). Used for arthritis, it is not. Exact same drug, exact same dose. Even aggressive chemotherapy drugs that can have really unpleasant side effects in humans often have far fewer side effects in dogs. (Cats are a different story.) And we have the huge advantage that if one of our patients does become sick on the chemo, we can just stop. At least we tried. The bottom line here is not to dismiss chemotherapy just because it's a scary word. It's not for every pet with cancer, but it is for some.

And finally, I am often asked about cause. People will say, "But we feed her the best food." Or they will ask about the lawn fertilizer or the water or the neighbour's treats. The truth is that none of these have any bearing. Cancer in pets (and in people, a few uniquely human high-risk behaviours excepted) is mostly due to three things: genetics, age and bad luck. The genetics is obvious as certain cancers are far more common in certain breeds. This doesn't mean that Fido's parents or siblings had to also have it for it to be genetic, it just means that the risk for an individual in that breed is higher, like playing with loaded dice. The age risk should also be obvious. As time goes on, your DNA accumulates damage and errors, like an old car or an old house, and some of that damage and some of those errors could lead to cancer. But the biggest factor is simply luck. The body of even the tiniest animal is inconceivably complex. When you begin to look at that complexity, it starts to seem amazing that diseases and disorders such as cancer aren't actually even more common. Be thankful for what works and don't be afraid of what doesn't. Sometimes it's not as bad as you think. Be like your pet and ignore the labels and words and just work to make each day as good as possible and then enjoy that day.

## MAKING THE DECISION

"I don't want him to suffer." Mr. Zielinski was looking at Prince, his 13-year-old German shepherd, as he said this.

Prince was breathing so heavily that it was almost the only thing he could do. He could barely walk a dozen slow steps before flopping down and heaving his chest again, his mouth half open. Mr. Zielinski was not a sentimental man. He had worked his entire life in a slaughterhouse and clearly prided himself on being practical and no-nonsense. But now his eyes were red, and his voice was barely above a whisper.

"No, I don't want him to suffer either," I said.

"And there is no hope, is there, doctor?"

No, there was no hope this time. Two years before, he had brought Prince in because he was very stiff and painful in the hind end. At that time he had also said that he didn't want Prince to suffer and had asked whether it would be best to just let him go. I examined Prince and decided that he likely had arthritis in his hips. I explained to Mr. Zielinski that I made euthanasia recommendations based on the answers to two questions. The first question is, is the patient's quality of life poor? In that case the answer was yes, Prince was in pain, and his quality of life was definitely poor. But the second question is, have we run out of realistic options that could provide reasonable hope for significantly improving that poor quality of life? That answer then was no. There was still reasonable hope as there were a number of realistic treatments for arthritis that we had not yet tried with Prince. Euthanasia is recommended when there is suffering with no hope. Two years ago, Prince had been suffering, so we alleviated the suffering with treatment. Now, however, he had a tumour on the surface of his heart that was bleeding into the space around his heart. He was suffering, and there was no reasonable hope of improvement. This time we would have to alleviate his suffering by letting him go. It was Mr. Zielinski's duty and my duty to do so.

Prince's case was reasonably black and white. Obviously an attempt should be made to treat arthritis in the hips before declaring the end of life, but an actively bleeding right atrial hemangiosarcoma is about as clear a signal that the time has come as one is ever going to get.

But what about the ones that are not as straightforward? These are unfortunately the majority, and it is a tremendous source of agony and indecision. So many pet owners have told me that the decision to put their pet down was the hardest decision they have ever had to make. In humans, it is out of our hands for the most part. Only with our pets do we have to routinely make a decision to end the life of a loved one. And it *is* routine. The average pet's life is only about a sixth as long as a human life, and, as discussed before, euthanasia is far more common than dying of so-called natural causes at home.

So how do we make this decision? As I mentioned, we look at quality of life and we look at hope. The hope part is usually a pretty easy medical question that your veterinarian can walk you through. The quality of life part is trickier though, especially in dogs and cats going through a gradual decline. Where do you draw that line? Quality of life is of course very subjective, but as a general guideline I think of the two A's: appetite and activity (or attitude, in pets that were not very active to begin with). I also look at a rough 48-hour rule. So, if for two consecutive days a pet who is known to be near the end of their life does not eat at all or hardly moves at all (or appears very depressed), it may be time. Also, as long as the hope question has been cleared up, trust your instincts — when you think it's time, it's probably time.

It is important that you be gentle with yourself. Do not agonize too much over picking the right day. There is often no such thing. As long we are in the ballpark, a few days, or even a few weeks, at the end of a pet's life doesn't matter to it. They have no sense of a tomorrow, or of how many tomorrows they want or should have. I have had many people comment later that, in retrospect, they think they waited too long. I have had nobody comment later that they think they did it too soon. Literally nobody. But our inability to let go is understandable, and it is human. Again, there is usually no perfect day. We all just do our best.

It's not easy, and it's never going to be easy. How could it possibly be? The best we can hope for is to not make it even more difficult than it already is. Fortunately once the decision is made, the actual act of euthanasia itself is almost always remarkably smooth and painless and swift. And so it was with Prince. Within minutes of making the decision, he was gone. Mr. Zielinski cried, telling me that he hadn't cried when his father died. He was heartbroken, but he had no regrets. Both he and Prince were at peace in their own ways.

# DO THEY KNOW IT'S CHRISTMAS?

The short answer is no.

The longer answer also features the word no but has more shading and nuance. But before I get into that let me reassure you (or warn you?) that this is not a typical veterinary Christmas essay. I will not be discussing the health hazards of chocolate and tinsel as you are all smart people and know this stuff already. Nor will I be discussing the moral hazards of forcing your cat to wear a little Santa suit or strapping reindeer antlers to your dog's head as I know I will not be able to dissuade you from doing so anyway. (It's an uncontrollable urge made worse by the advent of social media. Laws are needed. Personal essays are powerless against this urge.)

No, instead I will explore the question in the title. "Do they know it's Christmas?" No, they do not know it's Christmas, but they do know that *something* is up. And it makes them nervous. Now, to be fair, some of that something can be exciting and fun. Social dogs will enjoy sniffing the unusual people coming over, and self-confident cats will enjoy secretly licking the turkey. These are the exceptions though. Most pets are merely confused, and confusion leads to stress. Moreover, the majority of adult dogs and cats are deeply conservative (in the "small c" sense). Bliss for them is every day unfolding precisely like every day before it did. Bliss for them is the glorious routine. Everything. The. Same. Every. Day. *Everything!* You know this already. God forbid you get up at 7:05 instead of 7:00.

Christmas has the potential to mess with every element of this glorious routine. Furniture is moved. A giant tree is placed in the house and covered with myriad temptations you are forbidden to touch. A freaking giant tree! Festooned with shiny toys, for Pete's sake! Your walks are changed or — gasp — cancelled. Your mealtimes become more erratic. Random people come and go. Uncle Darryl keeps insisting that yes you do love to have your furry tummy rubbed, but you don't, and you bite him and people call *you* crazy. And your humans stay up late and sleep late. And all kinds of stuff is left lying around that you get yelled at for checking out. The list goes on. Christmas is stressful enough for many people, so just imagine how bizarre and unsettling it is for your dog or cat since they do not even know it's Christmas.

So what can you do? Cancel Christmas? Sure, go for it. Vet-approved. However, that's going to be unrealistic for most of you, so instead my recommendation is that you simply keep an eye on the importance of routine. Feed the same foods at the same times in the same amounts. Go for the same walks at as close to the same times as you can manage. *Keep scooping that litter box.* Set reminder alarms on your phone if you are worried you will forget or get distracted by the Christmas chaos.

And if you are going to put reindeer antlers on your dog, don't tell too many people, least of all your veterinarian.

## CAT GOES MAD

While I was hiking in England earlier this year, a headline in a small-town paper caught my eye: "COW BRUTALLY ATTACKS OAP." Yes, it was all caps. In fact, those four words were the only thing on the front page. (By the way, "OAP" means old age pensioner. I had to look it up.) In any case, it brought to mind a story Lorraine had told me about a similarly startling headline in the *Winnipeg Sun* when she was growing up. Apparently the front page screamed, "CAT GOES MAD," accompanied by a picture of a suitably concerned-looking elderly woman sitting on a couch festooned with doilies. And this got me thinking about rabies in cats. That's how that funky old train of thought sometimes goes. One minute you're thinking about OAPs, and the next you're thinking about feline rabies.

Rabid cats came so readily to mind because just prior to leaving for England, I'd had a telephone conversation with a client about the subject. As I outlined in a previous essay, I don't always have a minute-by-minute overview of my telephone messages. In fact, an hour or more can easily go by before I see them. On this particular morning, I opened the message centre on my computer to find a series of eye-catching messages from my receptionist:

*Please call Mr. Stirling. Thinks Buttons has rabies.*

*Urgent: Very concerned about his rabid cat.*
*Called again!*

Intrigued, I called Mr. Stirling back. "Hello. I understand you are worried that Buttons might have rabies?"

"Yes! She's not acting like herself at all!"

"How so? Can you describe what she is doing please?"

"Usually I keep the bedroom door closed at night, but two nights ago I left it open, and she came into my room in the middle of the night."

"Yes . . . ?"

"And then she jumped on me and sat there for a while. I woke up, but I didn't move. Then she bit me!"

"Oh dear. Did she break the skin?"

"No. I guess it was more of a nibble than a bite."

"Hmm. Anything else?"

"Yes! Then last night she did the same thing, except without the bite. That time she just purred loudly."

This was beginning to shape up like another Monty Python sketch. I have a great deal of faith in the shrewdness of my readership, so I'm confident you can more or less reconstruct my response and the rest of the conversation. No, Buttons did not have rabies. Buttons was bored and lonely and wanted to play. Mr. Stirling was relieved. He called back the next day to apologize for overreacting. There was no need to apologize. I would much rather people took rabies too seriously than not seriously enough, because that side of the coin is all too prevalent.

I am sometimes asked how many cases of rabies I have seen in my patients. The answer is zero. Shallow thinkers will take this as evidence that vaccination is not necessary. This is of course the wrong conclusion. The right conclusion is that it is evidence for the effectiveness of the vaccination program. Otherwise it's a bit like saying, "See, my house has never burnt down, so I can start letting the kids play with blowtorches." Countries without comprehensive rabies vaccination programs have shockingly high rates of the disease. Twenty thousand people die of rabies every year in India. *Twenty thousand people die.* It is one of the ugliest deaths imaginable. And the number of animals dying of it must be an order of magnitude higher.

So please, if you are at all concerned that your cat or dog (or cow) has gone mad, please do not hesitate to call. We won't laugh. (Unless you use a Michael Palin voice.)

❧ ❧ ❧

## WHEN THE SKY GOES BOOM

Norman sat beside Mr. Parker and looked at me expectantly. Expectantly because I had already given him three of his favourite liver treats. "If three, why not four, or even 14?" he seemed to be thinking. Regardless, he did not look especially nervous or anxious today. However, two days prior, this 30-kilogram Lab/border collie cross had put a dog-shaped hole in the Parkers' kitchen screen door. Then he'd run flat out for at least four kilometres, through the hammering rain and deepening mud. The Parkers found him several hours later, limping down a grid road, panting, bedraggled, exhausted. They brought him in to get him checked over because he still had a bit of a limp, and because they didn't want this to happen again. Norman had a storm phobia, and it was the start of the summer storm season.

Many dogs have storm phobias and noise phobias. These are actually two different things, although there is considerable overlap. About 90% of dogs with storm phobia also have a noise phobia, triggered by sudden loud sounds such as fireworks and cars backfiring. Curiously, the reverse is only true 75% of the time (noise phobic dogs who also have a storm phobia). Many also have other anxieties such as separation anxiety, but certainly a large number, like Norman, do not. There is evidence that storm-phobic dogs may also be reacting to the change in atmospheric pressure and to the flashing light in addition to the noise of the thunder. It is well known that dogs can hear the thunder approaching long before we do. This is a key part of the problem as many anxieties are worse when there is a wind-up anticipatory phase.

I talked to Mr. Parker about three types of solutions: training, tricks and drugs. Most of the time you have to use at least two out of the three. Norman needed all three.

Training is the best long-term solution if you can get it to work. The chances of success are higher if you can consistently put the time needed into it. That said, I don't judge people who are unable to. My own dog still chases cars, steals entire cakes and barks at the vacuum like it's the Antichrist. There are a few training approaches, but the one I like best is counter-conditioning. For this, find a long thunderstorm sound clip. Start to play it very quietly and briefly while feeding your dog treats or his meal. Keep it below the level that sparks anxiety. Over time, gradually increase the volume and duration, but always back off immediately if he shows any sign of being worried. You are trying to create a deep association between a temporary bad thing — storms — and a permanent good thing — food. For most dogs, the goodness of food will overpower the badness of storms, just so long as you take an extremely careful and gradual approach. This is best done well before storm season.

The tricks are fun. Get out your credit card and start surfing:

- There are Mutt Muffs, to block sound: www.SafeAndSoundPets.com.
- There are ThunderHuts, also to block sound: www.Thunder-Hut.com.
- There are Doggles, in case the lightning flashes are part of the problem: Shop.Doggles.com.
- And there are ThunderShirts, to calm by creating a secure feeling "hug": www.ThunderShirt.com.

Of these I have only seen the latter in action. My observation has been that the ThunderShirt seems to help many dogs, but that it's unusual for it to be the sole answer. Looks cool, though. Especially when matched with Doggles and Mutt Muffs. A cheap DIY solution is to let the dog tell you what reduces the noise and flashes for him. This means leaving all your (inside!) doors open and letting him find a bed to crawl under or a closet to stuff himself into.

And then finally the drugs. Some clients glaze over as I discuss all of the above and radiate a strong "just give me the drugs" vibe. There are several of these, but none are perfect, and all require you to be very watchful of the weather forecast as they won't work once the anxiety is already building up. It is good to have some medication on hand for when you know that a storm is predicted later in the day. Most drugs are given an hour or so before the expected onset of anxiety. In severe cases, it may even be worth having anti-anxiety meds prescribed to be given on a daily basis right through the storm season. Regardless, talk to your veterinarian as there is definitely no one-size-fits-all answer.

Ultimately, some counter-conditioning, a ThunderShirt and an alprazolam prescription were the ticket for Norman. He had a great summer — until they went camping in an aluminium trailer and were caught in a hailstorm . . .

## ELWOOD REGRETS NOTHING

Although he looked dejected, and although he would clearly rather have been somewhere else, in his heart I am sure that Elwood was defiant. He had done it before, and he would do it again. If his people left a Terry's Chocolate Orange lying in reach again, by George, he would snarf it down again before you could say, "Elwood! Drop it!" No question. Foil and all. It was so worth it for the three seconds the chocolatey goodness was in contact with his taste buds. Furthermore, it was his Christmas tradition, and tradition was clearly important to Elwood. Actually, I'm kidding — just access to anything remotely resembling food was important to Elwood. Forget tradition.

I showed the Sykes the chocolate toxicity calculator, which told us that 157 grams of milk chocolate in a ten-kilogram beagle translated into 35 milligrams of the active toxic ingredient per kilogram of beagle, which was in the "mildly toxic" range, likely to produce vomiting, diarrhea, shaking and an increased heart rate. Fortunately, we had only seen the first symptom, in part because the Sykes knew their Elwood and had rushed him in immediately after the futile "Elwood! Drop it!" so that we could induce vomiting and get as much out of him as possible. As an aside, I want you to know that although veterinary clinics can be awash in a potpourri of vile smelling substances, chocolate vomit holds a special place near the apex of the devil's perfumery. I mention this only so you know that the veterinary staff also suffers when you allow your dog access to chocolate. But I digress.

So chocolate is poisonous to dogs; this much most of you know. But do you know why it is poisonous? The aforementioned active toxic ingredient is theobromine, which is in the same methylxanthine class of stimulants as caffeine. What makes dogs different is that they metabolize it much more slowly than humans. Cats do too, but they are almost never interested in eating enough chocolate for it to matter as they can't appreciate the sweetness. Because it is a stimulant, at a high dose it can cause severe heart rhythm disturbances and potentially fatal seizures. At about 200 milligrams of theobromine per kilogram, 50% of untreated dogs will die. Theobromine content varies between types of chocolate, with milk chocolate having the least and baker's dark chocolate having the most. As a general rule of thumb, 28 grams (one ounce) of milk chocolate contains approximately 60 milligrams of theobromine while the same amount of dark chocolate contains about 200 milligrams, and baker's chocolate about 400 milligrams.

It may be of interest to note that a recent study of 230 vet clinics in England indicated that the risk of chocolate poisoning was four times higher at Christmas than any other time of year except Easter, when it was two times higher. Curiously, there was no increased risk on Valentine's Day or Halloween (although, mind you, the latter is a much smaller chocolate event in the UK than over here, and the former usually involves more expensive, closely guarded chocolates).

Incidentally, chocolate is theoretically poisonous in humans as well, although we are much less sensitive. A person my size would have to eat about four and a half kilograms of baker's dark chocolate, or an impressive 32.5 kilograms of milk chocolate, to be at significant risk of Death by Chocolate. I think that it is safe to predict that an array of increasingly distressing feelings would precede the fatal overdose and prevent you from getting to that point. But if not, imagine the obituary.

In the end it was not his zeal for foil-covered chocolate, or his sundry other dietary indiscretions, that did Elwood in, but rather an entirely unrelated kidney condition years later. I suppose he was in some way justified in his lack of regret.

## THE INEFFABLE WEIRDNESS
## OF DENTISTRY

A routine part of small animal practice is recommending dental work and then having the pet owner react as if you have just recommended Spanish guitar lessons for their dog or a set of encyclopedias for their cat. Some people view veterinary dentistry as evidence that we've gone too far in treating pets like people. These people (thankfully increasingly a minority, but a very annoying one) put it in the same category as pink leather jackets for chihuahuas and spa days for cats.

This can be true even when you show the client gum lesions that are exuding pus. Guaranteed, if you showed them lesions exuding pus anywhere else on the body, they would be horrified. They would expect immediate curative action. But not so for the teeth.

Why is this?

In part, it is because the teeth are generally not visible. That being said, I would like to note that sometimes the same people will then go on to show me a minuscule lump somewhere deep in the dog's groin or be genuinely concerned when blood tests reveal a more minor issue in an internal organ that is definitely not visible.

Another factor is that animals do not show dental pain. This sometimes results in the reverse problem wherein the client will absolutely insist the cat isn't eating because his teeth are bad. There are 968 common reasons for a cat not to eat, and that is not one of them. It is an uncommon reason for them not to eat. But the pain question is also only a partial answer as many other conditions that are not painful elicit far more interest from the dental-skeptical clients.

So then, what is my theory?

My theory is that we must blame the weird history of the human dental profession. Objectively speaking, teeth are part of your body. Actually, subjectively too. Teeth are part of your body: objectively, subjectively, factually. Agreed? Why then are they the only part of your body to have an entirely separate profession devoted to their care? It turns out to merely be an accident of history. We could have just as logically ended up with a separate profession focused on our fingers and toes. "I'm off to the digitist, dear!"

Before the 20th century, there was a division between physicians, who examined sick people and prescribed primarily quack remedies, and "barber surgeons," who used their sharp razors and steady hands to perform surgeries ranging from lancing boils to amputating limbs as a sideline between hair appointments. Some also had a set of pliers handy to pull teeth (as did some blacksmiths). That was the sum total of historical dentistry — yanking festering molars. Carpenters and other tradesmen made false teeth. As regulations began to gel, the more ambitious of the razor-wielding barber surgeons craved the prestige the physicians enjoyed, and those professions gradually merged, more or less accidentally, leaving tooth-pulling behind and unregulated. Later on the medical colleges who began to shut down all manner of other trades that were practising medicine without a licence (midwives come to mind) ignored the tooth-pullers because they didn't seem to be a threat and, some will darkly say, because they were of similar social backgrounds.

This has left us with a situation where in Canada, Medicare will pay to operate on your infected toe, but not to operate on your infected tooth. A situation where you have two incompatible sets of records regarding your health. A situation where some people see their teeth as being divorced from the big picture of their health. And for us poor veterinarians who have successfully kept the *entire body* of our patients under one umbrella, a situation where some pet owners have a different mental box for teeth than for the rest of Fido or Fluffy's body. Arbitrary and weird. Dentistry is weird.

P.S. My dentist is great and hardly weird at all. I just think if he were an MD dental specialist, my life as a veterinarian would be simpler.

❖ ❖ ❖

## FEELING TICKLISH?

I apologize for the egregious use of a lame pun as a title. I am defenceless against the ease with which one can make puns with the word "tick." Even the national veterinary association has launched a "Tick Talk" (I can hear your groans from here) awareness campaign, complete with an entirely over-the-top horror-themed ad. It's on YouTube if you're curious.

I imagine that you have already heard a fair bit about ticks and about the diseases they transmit, so I'm not going to repackage that information for you here. The Veterinary Partner website is a trustworthy resource if you have specific questions. Instead I'm going to highlight a less often discussed aspect that is alluded to in the title: ticks going on people. More specifically, ticks going from your dog onto you.

Ticks are potential vectors for disease. The word "vector" just means transporter, a kind of living vessel that carries a disease-causing organism from one animal to another. Most famously the deer, or black-legged, tick is a vector for the Borrelia organism that causes Lyme disease. But what we don't often consider is that your dog (and potentially, although quite rarely, your cat) could be a "vector for the vector," a kind of "metavector," to coin a term. Most people with tick-magnet dogs — you know, the dogs that disappear into the tall grass and come back with 20 ticks on them — are already familiar with the phenomenon of later finding ticks in the house, presumably having fallen off the dog. This could theoretically happen with any dog, particularly if they have darker or longer fur, as ticks can be very difficult to spot unless you are making a point of checking carefully. While I could find no studies that looked at the actual incidence of this, it is reasonable to assume that any dog could accidentally bring a deer tick home that could then infect you with Lyme disease. Eighty percent of humans who contract Lyme become ill, sometimes quite severely, whereas only about ten percent of dogs do.

And if that isn't enough to make your skin begin to crawl,* the less harmful but equally creepy brown dog

---

* Actually that crawling sensation you are feeling on your leg right now, or possibly in your scalp, is almost certainly not a tick as people generally can't feel them moving about. Sorry, I think I might have freaked you out.

tick can actually reproduce and complete its entire life cycle *inside your house*, causing a serious infestation. They like to crawl up walls and hang upside down. The good news for local readers here in Manitoba is that this type of tick is not, to the best of my knowledge, reported here (wood ticks, also called American dog ticks, are the other ones we see besides deer ticks), but we should remain alert as the American CDC considers the brown dog tick endemic in North Dakota and Minnesota, and it is common in Ontario.

Now I have totally freaked you out.

So let me conclude by trying to unfreak you. Fortunately this comes at a time when we finally have good tick medication. For years when people were concerned about ticks, we would more or less shrug and say something along the lines of, "well, you could try this, it helps a bit." In the last two or three years new products have come along that are easy to administer, very safe and far more effective than the previous generation. I'll leave the specific recommendations regarding which product is best for your dog to your veterinarian. None is 100% perfect, though, so I still recommend checking your dog over carefully after a walk on anything other than just the sidewalk. But at least now you have far less reason to feel . . . ticklish.

# THE BALLAD OF THE PRAIRIE FLEA

I'm willing to wager that if you were visiting your psychiatrist and he said, "What's the first word that comes to mind when I say 'dog'?" a reasonable percentage of you would say "fleas" (those of you who didn't say "bone," which is worthy of an essay on its own). Most cartoon dogs have fleas, and children tune ukuleles to "My Dog Has Fleas." An itchy dog is presumed by many to have fleas. But not so fast. Some of you reading this live on the Canadian Prairies or in the drier parts of the US, and woe betide the poor prairie or desert flea. You see, fleas love heat, and fleas especially love humidity. Consequently, there are many, many, many fleas in Tallahassee (hot, wet) and no fleas at all in Tuktoyaktuk (dry, cold). For better or worse Winnipeg, and the rest of the Prairies, is a lot more like Tuktoyaktuk than Tallahassee. Next time you're in Florida, pay attention to how many veterinary clinics you see. A lot, right? Fleas. It's all because of fleas.

Despite this ground truth the culture still teaches people to assume that an itchy dog or cat has fleas. It used to be the number-one myth I would bust. We would see the occasional case of fleas, perhaps two or three a year, versus the literally hundreds and hundreds of dogs and cats itchy because of allergies (yes, allergies — extremely common). I would marvel at this tough or perhaps misguided little prairie flea and wonder how she got here and what her plan for the winter was. A year ago this would have been a quick and simple essay to write — your pet does not have fleas. Done. This last fall, however . . . something has changed. They are still very rare, but we had perhaps eight or ten cases, quadruple the average. We're not becoming Tallahassee any time soon, but we seem to be inching a little closer. Add fleas to your running list of climate change consequences. Al Gore didn't warn us about this.

And how do you know your pet has fleas? Ideally you see the mighty flea itself, but they are tiny and astonishingly quick, and they are only on the animal to feed. The rest of the time they are — *gulp* — out and about in your house. Instead, we rely on a gross flea fact. Fleas drink blood and then poop out the digested blood. Consequently, flea poop looks like little black dirt particles in your pet's fur. Take one of these particles, place it on a white sheet of paper, wet it slightly and then streak it with your finger. If it streaks a rusty reddish brown, then you, my friend, have fleas in your house, and it is time for you to panic. No, I'm kidding — you should never panic, but you should be very slightly grossed out. (Note: cats may groom the flea dirt off, complicating matters somewhat.)

I won't go into treatment in any detail except to say, perhaps predictably, that you should talk to your veterinarian as it is a bit complicated. However, I will say a word about flea collars. That word is "useless." I have had clients come in and declare that the flea collar works well because Bozo doesn't have any fleas. This is akin to the man wearing the tinfoil hat declaring that it's working because aliens have not been able to zap him with mind-control beams. The prairie flea may have a little more swagger these days, but your pet would still have to be extraordinarily unlucky to encounter one. And if you're in Vancouver or Boston or London, or any other more humid part of the world, you'll be chuckling at all this. You know that your fleas have always had more than just a little swagger. They positively prance. No extraordinary bad luck required for your pets — just the ordinary garden variety.

## THERE ARE WORMS IN MY HEART

OK, not technically right in the heart itself, but more on that later. And not technically *my* heart — at least probably not — but more on that later too.

Spring is heartworm season in Manitoba and in much of North America, I think. Yes, it is. If you work in a veterinary clinic it is unmissable, unmistakable, unforgettable. It's not that our wards are packed full of dogs sick with heartworm disease; rather, it's that testing and prevention has to occur in a fairly narrow calendar window. Compounding this, for most people it's convenient to get all the other annual stuff done at the same time since they've dragged Fido in anyway (incidentally, no actual dogs are named

Fido, or Rover, or Rex, or Spot; some cats are though).
Consequently, most of us see as many patients in a week in
the spring as during a month in the winter.

I don't want to waste time spewing Basic Heartworm
Facts. You can get those from reputable corners of the
internet or, better still, from your friendly neighbourhood
veterinarian. Some of you even *are* your friendly neighbourhood veterinarian, in which case spewing would be
even more time-wasting. Instead I want to touch on a few
of the more unusual Cool Heartworm Facts. (OK, some of
you will consider these Gross Heartworm Facts, but I think
they're cool.)

COOL HEARTWORM FACT #1

Heartworm has probably been around forever (or such a
very long time that it may as well be forever) with possible
reports dating back to the 1500s. It was first positively
identified as such in 1847 in South America and then
in 1856 in the southeast USA. After that it continued
to spread north and west, arriving in Canada just over
a hundred years later. Now it is well established in the
southern parts of Ontario, Quebec and Manitoba, with
some cases also in BC's Okanagan Valley and in Atlantic
Canada. Nobody knows exactly whether it started in
South America or came there from elsewhere in the tropics
— possibly Africa — but it is now found on every conti-
nent except Antarctica, with the highest incidences being
in the hotter and wetter parts of the world.

## COOL HEARTWORM FACT #2

However, despite that spread, large areas of western North America and the Arctic do not have much of it yet. This is not necessarily because of a lack of mosquitoes, but because of a lack of positive dogs already there. Mosquitoes are just flying syringes moving heartworm from one dog to another. This is why the mosquito paradise of northern Manitoba is heartworm free. In the case of southern Manitoba, the population density in the corridor running south to Minnesota and on towards the Mississippi Valley is high enough to allow relatively easy dog-to-dog-to-dog transmission in a chain running south to north.

## COOL HEARTWORM FACT #3

Heartworms can be huge, up to 35 centimetres (14 inches) in length. And they can be numerous, with infestations of over 100 worms reported.

## COOL HEARTWORM FACT #4

The above-reported size and numbers are very rare, so most of the time "heartworm" is a misnomer. Most of the time the worms are hanging out in the pulmonary arteries leading away from the heart. Only if there are more than about 25 do they actually back up into the heart, and I have never seen that in my own practice. But "pulmonaryarteryworm," while more accurate, is so much more unwieldly. Unless you are German like me, in which case you prefer more accurate words, especially if they are long and unwieldly. However, I am sadly forced to admit that the Germans have failed us in this specific regard as heartworm in German is simply "Herzwurm." On the upside, though, the longest German word, nominated for "German Word of the Year" in 1999, is a semi-veterinary word! Rindfleischetikettierungsüberwachungsaufgabenübertragungsgesetz" means "a law to regulate the delegation of cattle marking and beef labelling." So there.

COOL HEARTWORM FACT #5
Wildlife can get heartworm. Logically foxes, coyotes and wolves are most at risk, but it has also been reported in bears, raccoons, leopards, sea lions and, oddly enough, beavers. Cats and ferrets are at some potential risk as well depending on where you live, so check with your veterinarian. Heartworm prefers dogs though, so higher numbers of worms are required to infect these non-dog species, and consequently, the risk is lower for them. A scary fact though is that heartworm in cats rarely produces symptoms and is most commonly only identified on autopsy of a cat who has died suddenly and unexpectedly.

COOL HEARTWORM FACT #6
Perhaps the coolest fact: humans can also get heartworm. Heartworm-positive mosquitoes bite us and release microfilaria (baby heartworms) into our bloodstream all the

time, but fortunately we are not good hosts, so 99.9% (and probably a few more nines after that) of the time, they die. However, there have been at least 80 cases reported in humans in the US, mostly in the lungs, but occasionally — shield your eyes if you are squeamish — in the eyes and the testicles (!). These have mostly been mild infections. The main problem is that on lung X-rays, a heartworm lesion looks very much like a tumour, prompting further invasive tests. Radiologists call it a "coin lesion." So if you overhear the interns whispering about this while they shoot sideways glances at you, politely clear your throat, put up your hand and ask about heartworm.

## A DOG'S MIND

"What do you suppose is going on in his mind?" Mr. Reynolds asked, smiling at Alf, his 12-year-old Lab cross. Alf sat patiently beside him, staring at me, not blinking, his eyes tracking my every move.

"We can only guess," I replied lamely as I leafed through Alf's file, trying to decipher the scribbles.

"He's totally focused on you. Paying close attention to everything you do. Watching to see if you reach for a needle or a treat!"

Focus, attention, watching. Fully conscious and aware. Mr. Reynolds was absolutely right, and it got me thinking.

For most of Western history we believed that animals were not conscious in the same way that humans were. We believed that they did not have a "mind." We believed that their behaviours were only the products of unthinking reflexes. In the 17th century René Descartes famously stated that an animal crying in pain did not actually feel it the way we did, no more than a machine felt the noisy grinding of gears. Denial of animal consciousness persisted deep into the 20th century. In fact, I am ashamed for my profession that up until the 1980s it was unusual for veterinary schools to teach much about pain control, in part because of lingering doubts regarding animal consciousness.

But here's the funny twist to the story: it is actually our own consciousness that we should be doubting.

Our species developed language that allowed us to organize complex societies, create astonishing technologies and, ultimately, conquer the world. However, this language ability lies like a heavy blanket on top of our consciousness, often smothering it. What we call "thinking" is often just a garbled torrent of words inside our head. Usually these words are just pointless rehashes of old conversations, rehearsals for future conversations, looping snatches of song lyrics, half remembered to-do lists, etc. Honestly, what was the last truly useful thought you had? Chances are it popped up unbidden in a rare quiet moment rather than out of the churning river of internal chatter.

Animals, on the other hand, do not have words. They do not plan conversations or construct lists of chores. They exist in a state of pure consciousness and pure awareness, with absolute focus and attention. Their minds are filled with what is right in front of them, right now. This is akin to what people who meditate attempt to achieve. Sure, memories and anticipations intrude for animals too, probably in the form of smell pictures, but far more than us they are present in the real world in real time, moment by moment, while we unconsciously drift along and then wonder where all the time went. Or wonder whether those last few traffic lights really were green.

I gave Alf both a needle and a treat. And then I went back to trying to figure out the file while wondering whether my next appointment was set up and what that thing was that I forgot to say and then remembered and then forgot again.

Alf was looking at the door.

# PART 4

# PECULIAR TALES FROM VETERINARY PRACTICE

## CONSIDER THE OSTRICH

Now consider the epileptic ostrich.

The three most common questions I am asked when someone finds out that I am a veterinarian are:

1) What is the most unusual animal you have treated?
2) How often do you get bit?
3) Do you know why my aunt's cat has a rash?

We'll ignore the third question, and I have already addressed the second, but the unusual animal question is actually worthy of a few commentaries, so let's start with the earliest one of those.

The first "unusual" animal I encountered in my career, aside from my girlfriend's deranged cat, was an ostrich. This goes back to my fourth year of veterinary school in Saskatoon. I no longer recall the ostrich's name, but for reasons that will become evident later, let's call him Johnny. Johnny had been brought in for examination and treatment because he was having seizures.

Now think about that for a moment.

A fully grown ostrich like the one in question is eight feet tall and weighs 300 pounds. This is much bigger than me. This is much bigger than you (pardon the presumption). Moreover, he has legs that can reach 14 feet in a single stride, claws the size of railroad spikes and muscle power enough to disembowel you. Disembowelment: now there's a hazard you don't consider too often. At the best of times, an ostrich has a brain smaller than its eyeball, but when it is seizuring, even that tiny speck of intelligence shuts down, and something akin to blindfolded chainsaw juggling ensues.

The professor told us to take off our lab coats before Johnny was brought in. "They like to peck at white things, like lab coat buttons," she said.

"Or like the whites of eyeballs," I thought.

Johnny was brought in by an assistant. We regarded him with nervous anticipation. He regarded us with . . . nothing. To our relief, Johnny did not appear to be in a disembowelling mood. His gaze was vacant and unfocused. The professor explained that they were medicating him to control his seizures and were still trying to work out the best dose. Consequently, one of his two functional brain cells was disabled.

"Now watch this," she said. The professor reached into her pocket and pulled out a marshmallow. Then she pulled a vial containing pills out of her other pocket, removed a pill and shoved it deep into the marshmallow. "Remember that they like to peck at white things?" She held the marshmallow out gingerly between her thumb and forefinger, and sure enough, with lightning speed, Johnny, who had seemed so stoned a moment before, lunged forward and gulped the marshmallow down in one impressively fluid motion. "And that, class, is how you medicate an ostrich."

I have had call to make use of this knowledge exactly zero times, but it is a cool thing to know. Johnny was led away again, and we shuffled off to go dissect something, each of us relieved not to have become an instructive ostrich attack statistic. Seriously. Ostriches are as dangerous as sharks. And sharks are rarely, if ever, brought into a veterinary clinic.

Incidentally, the most famous ostrich attack ever was the one on Johnny Cash in 1981. True story. In his autobiography, Cash recounts how he was almost disembowelled (there's that word again!) by his pet ostrich. He blames the incident for his subsequent addiction to painkillers. Yes, the world is a deeply weird place. You gotta love it.

In closing, if you are ever attacked, heed the words of President Theodore Roosevelt: "If, when assailed by the ostrich, the man stands erect, he is in great danger. But by the simple expedient of lying down, he escapes all danger." But lie on your stomach, Teddy.

## THE SMALLEST HEART

I had never before, and have never since, held in the palm of my hand something that felt simultaneously so powerful, yet so fragile. The hummingbird was hot, and it was fiercely alive, yet it could not move. The heat was astonishing. I knew that an animal with such a fast metabolism would have a high normal body temperature, but it was the first time I had felt anything like it. I stared at it, mesmerized by the jewelled green plumage on its wings, contrasting the shimmering purple-red of the throat. I could feel its small heart too, beating so quickly that it felt like the vibration of a tiny toy engine.

It was fourth-year veterinary school and I was on the small animal medicine rotation when someone rushed in this ruby-throated hummingbird that they had found lying on their patio. He (it was a he — the purple-red throat told us that) was tiny and far too light to register on any of the scales, but we estimated him to be about four grams, which is the weight of eight to twelve raisins. Consequently, the physical examination was cursory at best. Two interns, one resident and about a dozen students took turns peering at him, holding him gently and remarking on how hot — and how beautiful — he was. The consensus was that he had run into a window and injured his head. Whether he was just badly stunned or properly paralyzed was unclear. What was clear was that he was going to die regardless if we didn't feed him. When stressed, hummingbirds can starve to death in an hour because of their ridiculously high metabolic rates. I was given the task of feeding him and keeping him alive while the others busied themselves with the presumably more straightforward dogs and cats.

I found a stool in a quiet corner of the exam room and sat down with my miniscule charge. I looked at him carefully again, testing his wings and his legs, hoping perhaps that I might find something the others had missed. But no, he seemed physically to be in perfect shape. His little black eyes shone at me, and I imagined his terror but felt helpless to do anything about it. I set him in a dark box while I rummaged about for some instruments and high-concentration dextrose (sugar) solution. A technician then held him for me while I offered the dextrose, dabbing it on the end of his beak, but he didn't respond. He just kept staring at me. I then gently prised his long slender beak open and pulled his thin pink thread of a tongue out, which I had imagined would be rolled up inside like a window blind. (It wasn't.) I dipped his tongue in the dextrose and then, suddenly, there was some rapid flicking. He was drinking! It was the first movement we had seen from him. When he appeared to be done, I took him back in my hand while considering what else we could do.

The professor had been in her office when the hummingbird came in but was back now, and she came over to have a look at what we were doing. "Philipp, I hate to tell you this, but he's going to die no matter what you do." Her tone was kind, and I knew that she was probably right, but I somehow couldn't square it with the manifest intensity of the life that was cupped in my hand. "But keep doing what you're doing. Feed him every ten minutes or so. Keep him warm. And keep the cats away." She smiled and went on to help the other students with their patients.

I fed him three or four more times. Each time I opened the beak and carefully pulled out the tongue, and each time he drank vigorously for a few seconds and then stopped. The last time, his membranous grey third eyelids, which we had not seen before, suddenly came up, and that was it — he was dead. He was still hot, but the thrumming vibration of the heart had ceased, and he was limp.

The other students came by and joked that I had killed him, asking how I could kill such a beautiful thing, and I laughed along with them, but I was sad. I didn't cry, but I was very sad, and even today, almost three decades later, when I think about that hummingbird, it is with a mixture of wonder and sorrow.

## SPUNKY SWINGS LOW

Pity poor Spunky, the captive sugar glider. Pity his adorable big black eyes. Pity his cuddly soft grey fur. Pity his delightful cupped-handful size. Pity him because these features make him irresistible as a pet — a little plush toy come to vigorous life — and pity him because he does not want to be a pet. OK, "want" is a tricky concept in a creature with the brain the size of a chickpea. He is unlikely to be conscious of the fact that his kind lives in the forests of Australia, not the apartments of Canada, and he is unlikely to be conscious of the fact that his kind lives in large family groups of other sugar gliders, not in a household of enormous loud and smelly primates and possibly one or two four-legged predators. He is also unlikely to give much real thought to the problems inherent in wanting to be busy and noisy at night when the primates are sleeping, and then trying to sleep in the day when the primates are themselves busy and noisy. Even though he does not think about these things, there is no doubt that he would be far happier if he were ugly and were left alone to glide from eucalyptus tree to eucalyptus tree, with his family, at night.

Further pity poor Spunky, for I have been asked to castrate him. As with many cute and fluffy creatures, Spunky does not know that "cute and fluffy" also means "passive and gentle" to his primate captors. In his mind, he is fierce, and he is tough, and he has had it with you and all your BS. Tiny, cuddly creatures with big baby eyes can still bite hard. And these ones in particular can swoop down on you from above. His owners were members of the online sugar glider community and had tried all the recommended behavioural and environmental modifications, but at the end of the day, Spunky was still too . . . spunky.

The medical care of captive non-domesticated species can present the veterinarian with an ethical and moral quandary. My approach is to strongly discourage owner-ship of such animals but also to recognize that an animal like Spunky is now stuck with this situation as he cannot be released into the wild, so I have an obligation to do what I can to help make his life as pleasant as possible, under the circumstances. And on balance, in this case, it meant trying surgery.

So Spunky was presented on the appointed day, and the nurses handled him gently, gave him pain medication and then carefully induced general anaesthesia, at which point I was called into the O.R. for the procedure. While I had given the ethical and moral dimensions of this some considerable thought, I hadn't really done the same for the technical aspects. Neuters are, after all, really pretty similar from species to species.

Pretty similar except in sugar gliders, as it happens. They are marsupials, and marsupials are strange. And before I get angry emails from Australia, I don't mean strange in the pejorative sense. I mean it in the strict traditional sense of the word — unusual or surprising — as seen from the perspective of someone whose practice includes no marsupials at all. Except Spunky.

So what was so strange? His scrotum. Spunky's scrotum was strange. It dangled down between his hind legs on a long threadlike stalk like a teensy weensy little tetherball.

Now consider this carefully for a moment. Here is a creature that glides from tree to tree in the dark, presumably dodging twigs and branches, his scrotum dangling free beneath him all the while. Doesn't it strike you as problematic from an evolutionary perspective? Men reading this are feeling a little queasy now as they picture what must be a common mishap.

In any case, there he was, deep asleep, and there I was, scalpel in hand. I glanced at my nurse. She shrugged. I looked back at Spunky's scrotum and its breathtakingly long and narrow attachment. I will spare you the technical details, but ultimately, I had to abandon the normal approach, which involves a lot of careful dissection, transection and ligation, and instead . . . just lopped it off. I snipped the stalk, sewed it up and that was that. Ten minutes of pondering and ten seconds of actual surgery.

Somehow simultaneously both the easiest and the hardest neuter I have ever performed.

## FISH OF DEATH

Or at least "Fish of Extreme Pain."

Soon after I graduated, I decided to try to develop a sideline in fish medicine as way to make myself more useful to the practice. Or at least less useless. The sensible among you will immediately see the logical flaws in trying to get people to bring their pet fish into the clinic. There are several such flaws. But my employers, bless them, were indulgent and patient with me. To give myself some credit, I was nothing if not enthusiastic. I made sure I had the best textbooks, and I set to work writing brochures on a variety of fish health subjects. And then I waited for patients . . . and waited . . .

Until one day, the owner of a nearby pet shop came in carrying a large ice cream pail.

"What have you got in the bucket, Edna?"

"A fish! Actually, two of them."

Imagine my excitement. Just imagine it. I strode over to Edna and her bucket. Not walked, but strode. I peered into the bucket. Two fish indeed: a large, roughly eggplant-sized, colourful fish with bold orange and white stripes and long feather-like things sticking out all over it, and a small, roughly walnut-sized, dull brown–coloured fish. There were two really interesting things about this scene. The first was that the big fish was a lionfish. (More on why that's really interesting in a moment.) The second was that the little fish was headfirst halfway into the lionfish's mouth.

"Edna, that's a lionfish!"

"Yes, it's really expensive, and it's choking on that stupid catfish!"

Which fish was more stupid struck me as a debatable point. "I see . . ."

"Can you get the catfish out?"

"Um . . ."

So this is where I should explain what's really interesting about lionfish. Those cool-looking feathery things are actually sharp spines (easily sharp enough to slice exam gloves) and are covered in venom. The venom has an entertaining array of potential effects including, and I quote, "extreme pain, nausea, vomiting, fever, breathing difficulties, convulsions, dizziness, redness on the affected area, headache, numbness, paresthesia (pins and needles), heartburn, diarrhea and sweating. Rarely, such stings can cause temporary paralysis of the limbs, heart failure and even death." Well, only "rarely" death, so that's OK.

"Well, can you?"

"Um . . ."

The lionfish actually looked distressed. The catfish was presumably even more distressed, but it was hard to tell.

There was no way to grasp the lionfish without touching the venomous spines, and the standard aquarium wrangler's net wouldn't help, so, after a bit of pondering, I came up with an idea. I found two long pieces of wood — this was a while ago, so I don't remember exactly, but they might have been leftover molding from a reno — and a large pair of surgical forceps. I wielded the wood pieces with my left hand like giant chopsticks to restrain the lionfish while carefully submerging my right hand with the forceps to firmly grasp the tail of the catfish.

Deep breath.

Then I yanked.

The catfish was free! However, I am sad to report that it did not live to enjoy its freedom. The catfish immediately succumbed to its injuries, or to the shock of the whole unpleasant event. But the lionfish survived. And I survived. A mortality rate of only 33%. Not bad for a novice fish vet.

But that was pretty much the end of my short-lived career as a fish specialist.

Years later we were in the Cayman Islands and met a local with a boat full of lionfish. It turns out that they are an invasive and aggressive species that is decimating native fish populations. The government there was paying a bounty on them. And they are steadily spreading northwards.

## REALLY? ANYWHERE?

I had only been in practice for a year when a young woman who looked to be in her late teens came in with her cat, Loverboy. The first thing she said to me was that she only had 50 dollars that she had borrowed from a friend. She was living on her own on income assistance and could barely afford groceries. I told her that I could certainly examine Loverboy for that cost and that we could take it from there, depending on what I found.

Loverboy was a black and white boy. He reminded me a little bit of my first cat, Mook. He purred constantly through the exam and kept butting his head against my hand. But he was very thin, and his gums were very pale. The owner reported that his appetite and energy had been gradually declining over the last few weeks. He was only three years old, and she was very worried. I asked if he went outside and she said no, not now that they lived in an apartment, but a year ago they had been in a house, and he had then.

I stroked Loverboy and considered the options while asking a few more routine questions about his diet, his litterbox use, his general habits and so forth. He was clearly anemic, but the problem was that there were at least a half dozen possible causes that all needed different tests and all had different treatments. That being said, given that he had been outside before and was unvaccinated, I quickly formed a presumptive diagnosis: feline leukemia. This is a virus often transmitted between cats by fighting. One of its many potential effects is life-threatening anemia. I explained this to the owner, but she told me that no, he never fought — that's why his name was Loverboy. Also, when he had been going outside, it had always been supervised. Undeterred, I then explained that he could also have gotten the virus from his mother. The owner shook her head again and said that Loverboy's mother had been a very well looked after, fully vaccinated cat owned by her aunt.

Sometimes a diagnosis is so compelling and fits so neatly with what we see in the patient that our ability to process contrary information is impaired. Sometimes we are not as fully objective as we need to be. Fortunately this gets better with experience, especially after we have been burned a few times. But I was relatively new to this, and I insisted that my theory was correct and asked that she try to borrow another 30 dollars for the leukemia blood test to prove it, promising her that I was confident that this was the right thing to do. She reluctantly agreed and returned a few days later to have the test run. It was negative.

I was stunned — really stunned — and at a loss as to what to do next. She told me that she could not borrow any more money. Loverboy was still purring, still head-butting, but looking even weaker than the last time. I sent her home and told her I'd give her a call later that day after I'd had a chance to do some reading and to figure something out. But

I didn't read. I just sat at my desk and stared at the wall. I was going to have to ask my boss for help. Dr. C. had a reputation for having a sharp temper, and he definitely kept a very close eye on the practice financials, grumbling when we used disposable surgical needles rather than the ones that could be re-sterilized.

I explained the situation to him in detail. Dr. C. sat back in his big brown swivelling armchair and smiled at me. "Well, Philipp, you have a problem. You promised this young lady something when you should not have done so, and you did not listen to her very well. You're going to have to eat some crow now."

I nodded.

"I think this cat is probably bleeding internally, so give her a call back and apologize to her. Tell her that you've spoken to me and that I have approved an X-ray at no charge to her."

For the second time that day I was stunned. He never gave services away. Perhaps he was mellowing with age.

A few hours later Dr. C. and I were looking at the X-ray up on the viewer. I was stunned for the third time, and he for the first. There was a crisply defined oval object in the stomach, as bright white as bone. Squinting, you could make out something that almost looked like writing on it.

Dr. C. chuckled. "I guess I'm going to have to eat some crow too! This is a good opportunity for you to learn how to do a gastrotomy, Philipp. Tell the young lady that her cat needs surgery, and that we will do it at cost. She can pay us back at 20 dollars a month." Yes, he was definitely mellowing.

And so it came to pass that I was gowned and gloved and making an incision into Loverboy's stomach. I could feel the object, hard and flat. I eased it out of the stomach, wiped it off and held it up to look at in the strong surgery light. "It's copper!" I told Linda, the anaesthesia tech. "That explains it! He had copper poisoning causing the anemia! This will cure him. And there really is writing on it . . ." I handed it to Linda to wash it off more thoroughly.

She came back in in a minute, laughing. "It's one of those medallions you make in those machines that squash pennies. And it says — are you ready for this? It says, 'Good for a hug and a kiss, anytime, anywhere.'"

But possibly not in the stomach.

# FINNEGAN VS. THE POT ROAST

Humans divide everything they encounter in the world into categories. Dogs do so too. The difference is that humans use multiple sophisticated categories, slicing and dicing the world in the finest detail and then applying a bewildering array of hierarchical labels. Dogs, on the other hand, just use two broad categories: "food" and "not food." And I am here to tell you that the "food" category is breathtakingly wide. Now, to be honest, the "not food" category does have a few subcategories, such as "things to bark at" and "people who provide food," but really it is the distinction between edible and non-edible that they are most interested in. Food is everything. It is their passion. It is their god. This is especially true of puppies, and it is especially true of certain breeds.

Labrador retrievers and beagles are perhaps the most notorious of these breeds. The first time this principle was vividly demonstrated to me was with Billy Singh, a young male black Lab who came into the clinic one day a year or two after I graduated. He had been off his food for a couple of days, which was absolutely shocking to the owners. Billy would normally materialize out of thin air if they so much as lightly rustled a plastic bag, or if they even touched the drawer they kept the can opener in. But now he was just lying around looking sad. He would sniff at the treats they tried to entice him with, but then he would look away with an even sadder facial expression.

The diagnosis was gratifyingly simple for a relatively new graduate. There it was on the X-ray: a very dense, irregularly shaped object, about the size of a ping-pong ball, sitting in the small intestine. I showed the X-ray to Mr. Singh, who sighed and said, "That's a rock. Billy likes to eat rocks."

I didn't try to disguise my astonishment. "He likes to eat rocks?!" Since then, I have come to learn that rock eating is not all that unusual, but at that point, it was the first time I had heard of it. "Like, actually eat them? Not just play with them and then accidentally swallow them?"

"No, he eats them. Usually they just pass. I thought we had gotten rid of all the rocks in the yard, and we watch him like a hawk when we're on a walk, but I guess he found one somewhere."

"Wow, that's bad luck. It's a very specific size of rock that they can get down but then not easily pass all the way through. It looks like it's stuck there now. "

Mr. Singh didn't reply. He just sighed again and nodded.

The diagnosis was straightforward, and the treatment was straightforward too — Billy would need surgery. The surgery went well, and Billy recovered nicely. But none of this so far is the interesting part of the story. The interesting part of the story is that he did it again and had a second surgery a year later. And then about a half year after that, I got a phone call from Mr. Singh. (I'm sure you know where this is going.)

"Dr. Schott, you're not going to believe this, but Billy hasn't eaten in about three days."

"Oh no."

"I think he did it again. We're so careful, but I swear he's addicted. He must be able to smell those rocks a hundred yards away."

"It's unbelievable . . ."

"Look, we can't afford to keep doing surgery like this. And it can't be good for him either. Is there anything else we can do? Can you put a zipper in him?" Mr. Singh was chuckling, but it was a rueful chuckle.

"Ha! Good idea, but, um, no. I'm really sorry, but it does sound like surgery again."

These days it might be possible to consider using an endoscope, but none were available in Winnipeg then, and trying to drag large, rough objects back up the esophagus is probably not an ideal solution anyway. So Billy had a third surgery. Afterwards we decided that he would only be allowed outside, regardless of how well supervised, if he was wearing a basket-style muzzle that allowed him to pant, but not get his mouth around anything. And this did the trick. He went on to live a healthy, happy life with no further surgeries, although I'm sure he dreamed of tasty rocks to his dying day.

But as unusual as Billy's eating habits were, I have to give the crown for creative gluttony to dear old Finnegan Connolly.

Finnegan had demonstrated his mania for food early on. After he ate an entire loaf of bread, including its plastic bag, and then vomited it all up on their living room carpet, the Connollys became extremely careful about leaving food anywhere that might conceivably be accessible to him. But Finnegan was not discouraged. Finnegan worked diligently to broaden the definition of "accessible." Finnegan learned to open the refrigerator.

One Sunday morning he pawed it open, pulled the pot roast out and ate an astonishing proportion of it before anybody noticed. He vomited it up again, like with the loaf of bread, but this time he didn't stop vomiting. He kept on vomiting through the day, even when all that was left to come out was a bit of froth and bile. The Connollys became concerned and took him to the emergency clinic.

There he was diagnosed with pancreatitis, which is inflammation of a major digestive gland. Pancreatitis has a variety of causes, but a common one is when the digestive system is confronted with a sudden load of fat. Three-quarters of a pot roast is a lot of fat. It's probably the amount he would otherwise see in a month of kibble. Finnegan was hospitalized for several days on intravenous fluids and multiple medications.

The Connollys installed a latch on the fridge door.

Billy and Finnegan must have been soulmates. Both were persistent in their desire to eat what they shouldn't, and both were cunning in their persistence. Not long at all after what was widely referred to as "the fridge incident," Finnegan was back in the hospital again. This time he had managed to open the oven door, somehow knock the roast out without burning himself and then scarf the whole thing down. Open. The. Oven. Door. There are clients where I would have thought to myself, "Sure sure, the dog opened the oven door! You just don't want to admit that you left the roast out where he could reach it, but whatever." But the Connollys were serious people, and I had to believe them, as bizarre as the mental image was. It's not just the opening of the oven door, but also the maneuvering around the open door and then the getting of the pan and roast out. Maybe he used his mouth and paws? The mind truly boggles. A genius dog. A mad genius, though. Finnegan was hospitalized on intravenous fluids again, this time for even longer.

The Connollys installed a latch on the oven door.

There was no third pot roast incident, but Finnegan

was a "frequent flier" for the rest of his life, continuing to regularly find trouble, usually driven by his breathtaking appetite. The basket muzzle idea didn't work for him because he would howl and carry on any time they tried it, and as most of his indiscretions were indoors, he would have had to wear it constantly. Somehow, though, despite his self-destructive instincts, he managed to live a long time, gradually getting fatter, never losing his passion for food. In fact, while I don't remember why or how he died, I do remember being told that he kept on eating to the very end.

## "NASTY, BIG, POINTY TEETH"

Yes, another Monty Python reference. The Python fans among you will immediately recognize from the title that I'm going to write about rabbits today. And not just any rabbits. Not the fluffy, gentle, innocent rabbits almost everyone imagines. No, I'm going to write about the vicious ones. Vicious rabbits? How is that possible, you ask? Remember this — the rabbit has no idea that he looks cute and cuddly and harmless to a human. He may seem a nervous, timid creature much of the time because he is a prey species after all, but in an environment where he has learned to become confident, his true warrior self may emerge. As evidence, I offer the following telephone conversation I had with a client a few years ago:

"Dr. Schott, thank you for coming to the phone right away. I'm calling from my bedroom," said Ms. Fitzsimmons.

This seemed like an unnecessary detail. I became faintly alarmed. "Yes?" I offered cautiously.

"It's Mr. Cuddles, I don't know what's wrong with him!"

Mr. Cuddles was a small floppy-eared grey rabbit that she had had for about a year. Relieved, I asked, "What symptoms are you seeing?"

"He's gone crazy!"

"Oh? What is he doing that seems crazy?"

"My bedroom is at the end of the hall where his little house is. He won't let me past his house!"

"Won't let you past?"

"Yes! He attacks me and bites me!"

"Um . . . how long has this been going on?"

"All morning! He just gets madder and madder every time I try! I don't know what to do! I need to get out! What's wrong with him?"

What was wrong with Mr. Cuddles? Nothing really. He was just a highly territorial male rabbit, allowed to roam free, whose "lair" had been set up in the hallway. With time he became confident enough to defend his lair. I told Ms. Fitzsimmons to come out of her room holding a blanket in front of her and then to toss the blanket onto Mr. Cuddles so that she could quickly sprint past. I told her that once things settled down, she should wait until he was sleeping in his house and then scoop him up with a towel, put him in a cage and bring him in to be neutered. Neutering doesn't always help, but in this case, taking the testosterone out of him plus moving his house to a far corner of an unused room seemed to do the trick.

The words of Leo Tolstoy come to mind: "It is amazing how complete is the delusion that beauty is goodness." Or, in case of killer rabbits: "It is amazing how complete is the delusion that cuteness is innocence."

## PETTY CHEW

Before I begin, I want to emphasize that this is very much a "don't try this at home" scenario. What happened here was unique, and I don't expect ever to see this work again. Not only was the outcome unique, but so were both the patient and the owner. Actually, I should call him the guardian, not the owner. You'll see why.

It was a sunny September afternoon maybe 15 years ago. I spotted an older gentleman in the crowded waiting room, wearing a battered, grease-stained parka despite the relatively warm weather. He was holding a cardboard mandarin orange box on his lap. According to the appointment schedule, his name was Ray Thibodeau, and he was bringing me a rabbit named "Petty Chew" to examine. The receptionists were busy, so I got an exam room ready and ushered him in.

After hellos and introductions and handshakes I asked, "So, who have we got in the box here?" The name seemed odd, so I wanted to be sure.

I couldn't make out Mr. Thibodeau's answer as he spoke very quietly with a thick Franco-Manitoban accent and had, as his smile revealed, quite a few missing teeth muddling his enunciation. "Pardon me?"

He smiled a huge gap-toothed smile, laughed and said the name again, louder this time. This time I heard "Petit Chou." Mr. Thibodeau added, "Sometime I call 'im PC."

"Ah, Petit Chou! Little cabbage! The receptionist put it down as 'Petty Chew.' That makes more sense now. That's a great name! But PC might be easier. Let's have a look at him then." I opened the box and peered inside. PC was not an ordinary pet bunny. PC was a wild rabbit. To be precise, he was a young Eastern Cottontail. To be even more precise, he was a young Eastern Cottontail with his left hind leg wrapped up in a big gauze and tape bandage.

"'E break 'is leg," Mr. Thibodeau said.

"I see," I said quietly and began to move my hands over the surprisingly calm-looking rabbit. Wild rabbits never survive in captivity. As a prey species they are pro-grammed to be terrified of potential predators, so close interaction with humans leads them to have a non-stop interior monologue of "OMG! OMG! OMG!" And then they actually die of the stress. All of them. Usually pretty quickly too. PC was obviously still in a state of shock from having been picked up.

"Can you give 'im an X-ray?" he asked after I had finished my cursory examination and closed the box.

"Well, I suppose, but I'm sorry to tell you that this is not going to end well. It's wonderful that you want to help him, but the poor little bunny is not going to survive. They never do. He is still in a state of shock that masks his extreme distress. The kindest thing is to put him to sleep."

Mr. Thibodeau considered this for a moment and then, speaking slowly and loudly so that he was sure I would understand, said, "But I 'ave 'im a mont' already. I fix 'is leg. But I want to know 'ow it look on de X-ray now an' if de bandage can come off."

One of the great things about this job is its seemingly boundless capacity for serving up surprise. This was a surprise. I looked at him blankly. "A month?"

"Yes, a mont' an' a few day."

"And you put this splint on yourself? And he's eating and pooping normally and moving around?" I still couldn't wrap my head around this.

"Oh yes! Petit Chou is doing very well! We are big friends now. I 'ave to talk wit' 'im gentle an' quiet at firs' so 'e will let me 'elp 'im, but then 'e understan' me an' 'e let me."

I blinked rapidly. "Um, OK then. Well, sure . . . let's do an X-ray. Just so you know, it'll cost about a hundred dollars." He nodded and began pulling a roll of twenties out of his shirt pocket. "No, no, it's OK, you don't pay me now! Pay at reception after."

In the X-ray room the technologist and I marvelled at PC's bandage splint. It was thick enough to provide support, but not so thick that it was excessively cumbersome. It wasn't perfect, but to be frank, it was better than many of the ones I've seen applied by newly graduated veterinarians. And then we further marvelled at the X-ray. There it was — a clean fracture of the tibia, nicely aligned and showing excellent signs of healing. I called Mr. Thibodeau in, showed him the X-ray and congratulated him on doing an excellent job. I told him that the splint could come off in a couple weeks, and then he should look at releasing him back into the wild.

Right on schedule he came back two weeks later, and, sure enough, PC's leg was healed enough to allow us to remove the splint.

About two months later Mr. Thibodeau was back in the waiting room with that mandarin orange box on his lap again. "Oh no," I thought. "Another one. And he's not going to be so lucky two times in a row."

"I bring Petit Chou for a check-up!" Mr. Thibodeau said when he set the box on the exam table. "'E is doing really good, but I want to be sure."

"You didn't release him?"

"Yes, I do, but 'e keep coming back! 'E wait by de door! And now is winter soon, so 'e come inside wit' me."

I really debated about publishing this story because I didn't want people to get the wrong idea. If you find a rabbit with fur and with eyes open, no matter how small, young and alone looking, leave it alone! Often baby rabbits that appear to be orphaned are not. Petit Chou was different because he had an obviously broken leg. And honestly, if he had been brought to me right away, I would have euthanized him. But there was something extraordinary about Petit Chou, and he reminded me to be very careful about prejudging patients. And there was something extraordinary about Mr. Thibodeau, and he reminded me to be very careful about prejudging people.

Every veterinarian has had the experience of a well-groomed and well-dressed client who pulls up in a luxury car and then gets angry over a relatively minor expense and threatens to euthanize or abandon the animal. And every veterinarian has had the experience of a client who looks and sounds like a homeless person who then moves heaven and earth to do everything possible for an animal. Our reflex to prejudge is powerful, but often so counter-productive.

Petit Chou/PC/Petty Chew (the file stayed under that name) went on to live at least two more years with Mr. Thibodeau, hanging out in his yard just outside the city and coming in during bad weather and through the winter. He came to the clinic for occasional check-ups and always looked good and always looked calm. Then the visits stopped, and I don't know what eventually happened to him. When it occurred to me to call to find out, the number was out of service.

# WHAT THE SEEING EYE DOG SAW

A little factoid that people have occasionally quoted to me
is that the average dog is about as smart as the average
two-year-old child. Google it; you'll see many references.
But as with many Google-friendly factoids, it is silly. It
is a soundbite oversimplification of complicated science.
In fact, the specific research paper that gave birth to this
idea only demonstrated that the average dog recognized as
many words as the average two-year-old. English words,
mind you, not dog words. This actually makes the average
dog seem astonishingly smart to me. Especially since my
own dog sometimes seems to recognize as many words as
a cucumber does (but he's very handsome).

There is no doubt that human intelligence is extremely
broad compared to dog intelligence. Our own intelligence
applies itself vigorously to taxes and fashion and phi-
losophy and physics and indoor plumbing and why the
freaking OS update won't install properly and a million
more things. Dog intelligence is not nearly as broad, but
where it needs to be, it is exceptionally deep. Whenever
I think about smart dogs, I think about one particular
patient, Sierra McNabb.

Sierra was a Seeing Eye dog. She was a golden retriever
from central casting — the kind you see in happy suburban
family advertisements for life insurance and Jeep Grand

Cherokees. She belonged to Roger McNabb, a spirited single older gentleman, also from central casting — the kind you see at the bar telling boisterous jokes to the bartender and buying rounds for strangers. Roger had not been fully blind that long, and Sierra was his first guide dog. He had flown out east to meet her and to go through the final stages of the training with her. It goes without saying (although watch me say it anyway) that they were inseparable and that she was indispensable to him. Sierra knew how to guide him to the post office, to his doctor's office, to the 7-Eleven and, my favourite, not just to the liquor store, but right to the specific location in the specific aisle where Roger's favourite whisky was. Not just a smart dog, but a useful dog. Try to get your two-year-old to do that for you.

One incident made it clear to me, however, that there was a deeper thought process at play with Sierra rather than just a robotic response to commands. As with 95% of golden retrievers, Sierra had recurrent ear infections. Those infected ears were very sore, and Sierra hated having them handled and looked at. She would sit obediently enough and permit the examination, but her eyes said, "Why do you keep doing this? Don't you know by now what's wrong, you fool?"

One day Roger was due to bring her in at 10:00 a.m. He lived within walking distance and was always very punctual, making allowances for weather or anything that might slow them down. By 10:10 I was already a little concerned. The receptionist called his home, but there was no answer. Just then we noticed Sierra and Roger walk past on the sidewalk out front. Sierra took a quick furtive glance at the door, but kept moving ahead. A moment later they came back, walking the other way, again right past the door. The receptionist ran out to get them.

Roger was flustered, "I count blocks and I knew we had gone too far, so I turned her around. We went back and forth like that four times! I don't know what got into her; I know she would have seen the door. I've never known her to be so confused."

Confused? Hardly. Sierra and I exchanged the most fleeting of glances: she knew that I knew that she knew. From that day forward, we would keep a careful lookout at the door when Sierra and Roger were due.

## LEROY AND THE SOMBRERO

"How long? How long has he got?" Lisa was struggling not to cry.

"It's really hard to say. Every cat is different, but not long, I'm afraid. Maybe four to six weeks." I briefly averted my eyes when I said this. These are always horrible conversations to have to have, but Lisa was a friend, so it was even worse.

She gasped a quiet "no . . ."

"I'm so sorry, Lisa." I put my hand on her shoulder.

Leroy seemed supremely unconcerned by all of this and was attending to the important business of licking the ultrasound gel off his chest. Lisa and I kept staring at the screen, where a short video clip of Leroy's heart was looping continuously. I had only been doing ultrasound for three or four years, but I had already seen at least a hundred normal hearts, which was enough to know that this one was profoundly different. In fact this was possibly the most abnormal heart I had seen so far. The two chambers that pump the blood out of the heart, called ventricles, were misshapen and contracting spastically, and the two chambers that receive the blood into the heart, called atria, were ballooned out to at least three times their normal size because of the backup from the flailing ventricles. Even a lay person who had never seen a heart ultrasound before could easily appreciate that this looked bad.

For serious and life-threatening diseases, deciding on prognosis is often more difficult than deciding on diagnosis and treatment. Coming up with Leroy's diagnosis was easy — restrictive cardiomyopathy — and his treatment was sadly easy too — not much other than symptomatic relief — but his prognosis was impossible to determine with confidence. Often there are no studies at all to guide you, so you are left in the position of having to give the client an educated guess based on what you know about how aggressive a disease usually is, and based on your past personal experience with it.

As it happened, just a week prior, I had had the horrifying experience of watching a little dog's heart rupture live on the ultrasound screen. One of his atria had become so distended and stretched out that in the middle of the ultrasound examination, it developed a tear in its outer wall and began to rapidly bleed out into the space around the heart. I had never seen that before, or frankly even imagined it happening. He lost blood pressure so quickly that he just slumped. The owner began to scream — "What's happening! What's happening!" — while I struggled first to comprehend it myself and second to find a way to quickly and clearly explain it to her. Even though I knew it was hopeless, we rushed him into the treatment area where we kept the emergency supplies. There was nothing we could do. I know that I couldn't have prevented it either because he came to me that sick, but I felt absolutely horrible nonetheless. All these years later I can still clearly hear the poor woman's screams in my mind's ear. At least the dog didn't suffer because he instantly blacked out when this happened.

Even though that dog had an entirely different disease than Leroy, they both ended up with extremely dilated atria. I'm sure this fresh memory coloured my estimation of Leroy's prognosis. However, I did go on to explain that prognosis is almost always on a bell curve. I told her that the majority of patients that look like this on ultrasound cluster around an average prognosis of four to six weeks, but there are a small minority at either edge of the bell who go a little quicker than expected on the one side or manage to survive a bit longer on the other. What I didn't really have a clear grasp of at that point in my career was how much the shape of the bell varies. In fact, for cats with cardiomyopathies, it looks less like a bell and more like a sombrero. Sure, there are quite a few patients who hang out in the average zone represented by the crown of the sombrero, but the brim is very wide in all directions, with room for plenty of cats. Some unfortunately do very poorly and die quickly, and some, who look exactly the same on any test you care to administer, do very well and live well beyond the average. Nobody knows why.

No doubt you've guessed by now that Leroy's heart kept ticking past the four to six weeks. In fact, Leroy made it all the way out to the far edge of that sombrero brim and lived two more years. I was amazed, absolutely amazed. But people who had a deeper respect for the old saying that cats have nine lives just smiled and nodded. You just never know which of those lives they're currently on.

## A THING I AM TERRIBLE AT

The appointment looked innocent enough: "3:00 — 'Count Basie' Simmons — collect sample." I did wonder briefly what sort of sample, but figured it was probably a needle biopsy of a lump as the techs do all the blood draws.

I entered the room and introduced myself to the owners, an older couple, he sporting a Tilley hat and a bushy white moustache, and she elegantly turned out and clutching a red notebook with "Count Basie" written boldly on the cover. Smiles and solid handshakes all around. There were two dogs in the room, both rough collies (*Lassie* dogs, in case you're not sure).

"The Count has a friend along for moral support," I said, chuckling lightly. I crouched down and invited them both to sniff me.

"In a manner of speaking," Mrs. Simmons replied, also chuckling lightly. "Ella is his teaser."

Uh oh.

"Teaser . . ." My heart dropped. I knew what I was collecting. Ella and the Count seemed relaxed about the whole thing. Mr. and Mrs. Simmons smiled at me. Obviously, it was my turn to say something. "So. Um. I am just collecting for analysis, then? Or are we . . . um . . . using it?"

"To analyze, please. He's been a bit of a dud, I'm afraid. Such good bloodlines, but no luck so far." Mrs. Simmons said this in a pleasant, matter-of-fact tone.

"They said you were the best!" Mr. Simmons added enthusiastically.

I made a mental note to track down the comedian who told them this. It's not that I am in any way embarrassed by the procedure (I *am* a doctor), it's just that I am not good at it. In fact I am terrible at manually ejaculating dogs. For example, there was that time with the pretty young woman and her toy poodle stud, Robert. God.

But I knew what to do. I excused myself to "get what I need," which in fact was mostly just a few deep breaths and a couple minutes to quickly scan the net and the books for tips. It is not, as the saying goes, rocket science. The procedure is essentially what you imagine it to be. Although a cool dog penis fact, if you didn't know this already, is that it contains a long bone, the "os penis." For real. This makes things easier in some ways. I'll leave the obvious jokes to you.

I stepped back into the room. Gloves, lube, collection vials. Everything ready. I looked at Count Basie, and he looked at me. Mr. and Mrs. Simmons smiled encouragingly. I made sure that Count Basie had sniffed Ella, who was apparently just coming into season, and then he and I began.

[Fade out for the sake of decorum.]

It wasn't working. Mr. Simmons offered, "Maybe the white coat is putting him off?" I took it off, vowing to myself that that was as far as I would go.

It still wasn't working. I kept trying, varying rhythm and pressure from time to time, reapplying lube, trying to look relaxed and professional, but the Count just stood there, panting, not even glancing at me. My hand was getting tired.

"Oh dear," Mrs. Simmons said and wrote something in her notebook.

I was determined to succeed this time, but my hand was really beginning to cramp, and Count Basie remained as unmoved as a blind man at a Van Gogh exhibit. "I'm sorry, but this just doesn't seem to be the day," I said weakly.

"Don't feel bad, this happened to the last vet too."

I booked them to try again in a week when Ella was more in season. I knew I'd be away then, so they'd have to see my colleague. "He really is the best at this," I assured them, smiling a wicked little smile to myself.

*᛫ ᛫ ᛫*

## EDWARD'S REALLY BAD DAY

I imagine that this will come as a surprise to you, but the worst day of Edward's life was not the day we cut his penis off. No, it was the day before. The day before we cut his penis off, Edward tried to pass a very small bladder stone. But it was not small enough. It made it into his urethra, but not out again. Consequently, he could not pee, and consequently, he was having an increasingly bad day until it became the worst day of his life.

First thing the next day Mrs. Heinzel brought the poor howling Edward in. He was a large, sandy-coloured cat, the third in a series of large, sandy-coloured cats the Heinzels had owned. His bladder was the size of a Texas grapefruit. We quickly anaesthetized him and attempted to pass a catheter, but no amount of coaxing and flushing on our part could get the little stone to budge. Crystals are a common cause of urinary obstruction and are generally fairly easy to dislodge, but this was different. The only solution was going to be to perform a perineal urethrostomy (cut his penis off) and anatomically turn him into a female with a wider urethra. Females almost never obstruct.

Mr. Heinzel had recently died, and Mrs. Heinzel didn't drive. Their son lived in Winnipeg, so he was often able to bring Edward and Mrs. Heinzel to the clinic, but it was sometimes difficult to fit into his schedule and sometimes impossible, in which case she used taxis.

Around this time Edward began to hate me. He had always been a bit of a hisser but had been manageable with a calm and slow approach. But since his procedure he had become more or less unmanageable. I don't think he blamed me for his sex reassignment, but he almost certainly blamed me for the hospital stay that followed and all the attendant injecting, pilling, temperature taking, close examining and other undignified manipulations. Because of the increasing difficulty with transportation, and because I hoped that Edward's hatred of me was connected to the clinic, I offered to start doing house calls. We don't advertise house calls because there is no way to make it financially viable to have a doctor and a tech out of the building for a span of time during which they could see three or four patients in the clinic, but for special clients and with enough notice, we will occasionally do it. And in fact I like it as it feels like a break to do a little driving and to get away from the ringing phones, barking dogs and, at times, frenzied staff.

But Edward still hated me. The first time we went to Mrs. Heinzel's house he came up to the front hall to greet us, took a few sniffs of my extended hand and began to hiss. Sigh. But Mrs. Heinzel really appreciated the house call, so even once Edward no longer had any immediate medical needs, I still went to her house once a year for his regular annual check-up and vaccinations. It became part of my springtime routine. I became familiar with the potholes and the ice ruts of her West End street, but every year I forgot which way to drive down the street in order to be able to park, and the March ruts were so deep that I couldn't turn my little Beetle around to face the right way. The tech would come along with a thick blanket and heavy leather gloves to hold Edward on the small kitchen table while I performed what can at best be described as a cursory examination while he screamed at us and attempted to flay us with his claws. All the while, Mrs. Heinzel would chuckle, "Oh Edward, you're such a bad boy." But from her smile it was clear that she didn't mean it.

As the years went by Mrs. Heinzel became more and more stooped and wizened while Edward became more and more rotund. He was gaining at the pace of roughly a pound a year. When I pointed this out as gently as I could, Mrs. Heinzel would chuckle again, "Oh Edward, he's such a bad boy." Then one year he lost weight — quite a bit of weight, in fact. While he shrieked at us, I explained to Mrs. Heinzel what the possible causes could be. I told her that the best thing would be for us to take him back to the clinic with us for tests as there was no way we were going to be able to get blood samples from him at home and, in any case, he might need an X-ray or an ultrasound.

After the tech and I wrestled Edward into his travel kennel and the tech left to bring some of the equipment out to the car first, Mrs. Heinzel turned to me and said, "I don't know how much longer I'm going to be around, or, from the looks of things, how much longer Edward is either, so I wanted to tell you this now while I have the chance." She paused, looked me in the eye and then chuckled one of her trademark chuckles. "Edward and I were made for each other. When I was a baby, they couldn't figure out whether I was a boy or a girl. I had both parts until they decided to make me a girl. So, we're a real pair, Edward and I."

I cannot overstate how extraordinary this sounded coming out of the mouth of a someone who looked like a sweet old granny from a vintage television show. It was yet another occasion in my life when I was left fumbling for an appropriate response. "Oh my," was the best I could come up with. She just smiled and patted my arm.

Edward's problem ended up not being immediately life threatening, and they both lived for a little while yet. He hated me until his dying day. After Mrs. Heinzel died, her family gave me a lovely pencil sketch of Edward, which hangs above my desk to this day, glaring at me. I think he's trying to teach me something, although I'm still not sure what.

## SNIFF THE TEDDY

Ms. Baker was a great client — one of those you wish you could clone. She always asked intelligent questions, always listened carefully to my advice and was always cheerful. Moreover, her dog, Rumpelstiltskin — Rumpel for short — was a very sweet little poodle cross who was a pleasure to look after. I would guess that Ms. Baker was in late middle age, and I knew that she lived alone. She lived in a small apartment not far from the clinic, one of the few that still allowed dogs. And Ms. Baker was absolutely devoted to Rumpel. It was obvious that he was the sun around which the planets of her life revolved, yet she managed somehow not to spoil him either. In any case, it was a true love story, so when Rumpel eventually died, she was absolutely stricken with grief.

About four months after Rumpel's passing, I saw that Ms. Baker was my next appointment, but without a new pet, so I assumed that she had come to ask my advice about when and how to consider getting another dog. When I came into the exam room I could see that she had a laptop and a large plastic shopping bag. We greeted each other warmly, and I expressed my condolences again on Rumpel's passing. Ms. Baker then told me that she wanted to show me some pictures of him and proceeded to start up a slideshow on her laptop. There must have been close to a hundred photos of Rumpel, slowly and artistically fading one to the next, set to soft piano music. It was heartbreaking, but honestly, after the first 30 or 40, I was becoming a little anxious about how long this was taking and, moreover, I was starting to steal sideways glances at the shopping bag. Home baking for me? Big box of chocolates? Bottle of wine? It's a terrible thing to admit, but it's true.

The slideshow eventually ended, and I told her what a lovely tribute it was. Then she reached into the bag. I leaned forward. She pulled out a battered old teddy bear with one button eye dangling from a thread and an ear missing. More or less the opposite of a bottle of wine.

"Dr. Schott, I have to ask you something very important."

"Yes, please do."

"Can you tell different species apart by the smell of their urine?"

This was not what I was expecting. Wondering where this could possibly be going, I answered cautiously, "Um, well, I don't think I can tell neutered and spayed cats and dogs apart that easily, but the smell of an un-neutered cat's pee is quite distinctive."

"What about rodents?"

"Oh, well, that's not so hard." Warming to my subject, I went on, "Rats and mice have unique urine odours, as do guinea pigs and rabbits, although rabbits are not technically rodents."

"That's terrific!" Ms. Baker was beaming. I was still completely baffled. Then she held the teddy bear out towards me. "This was Rumpel's favourite toy. Can you sniff it for me please, and tell me if you smell mouse pee?"

OK, a little odd to be sure, but she's upset that mice might be peeing on her beloved dog's teddy. Fair enough. I gamely took the bear. It was a bit damp all over. "That's a lot of mice," I thought. I took a cautious sniff. Faintly urinous. But definitely not rodent urine. Then I blotted the bear with a piece of paper towel. Yes, it did look like pee.

"It does seem to be urine, but I'm sure it's not mice, Ms. Baker." I was proud of my deduction.

"That's wonderful! Thank you so much! I'm so relieved!"

I clearly looked perplexed, so she went on.

"See, Dr. Schott, I was really hoping that it wasn't mice because that means that it was Rumpel!"

"Ah . . ." was all I could manage.

"He's come back! Rumpel used to pee on his teddy all the time. He loved it so much. It makes me feel so good that he's back! Now I can lay in bed at night and know that Rumpel is down there enjoying his teddy like he always did."

There really is no way to respond to something like this. I made a few "oh" and "huh" noises and then gently guided the conversation to how she was doing and whether she had looked into grief counselling. She left, smiling and visibly elated. I shook my head sadly and thought, "Poor woman, she's snapped."

That evening I told my wife, Lorraine, the story. She listened attentively, appropriately astonished at the right moments, and then when I was done she looked me square in the eyes and was quiet for a long moment. "Philipp, you know who was peeing on that teddy." It was more a statement than a question.

"No, funny, I hadn't actually thought about it because the whole scenario was so bizarre." But now I began to feel a faint tingle of unease run through my brain.

"It's obvious. It was her."

I used to tell this story a lot, and I enjoyed telling it because it invariably got a strong reaction — gasps of horror or shrieks of hilarity or both, depending on the crowd. But as time goes on it somehow makes me sadder. I don't tell it very often anymore.

## HE ATE WHAT?!

Dogs and cats, but especially dogs, will eat all manner of bizarre things. I have already introduced you to Billy the Lab, who on three separate occasions ate rocks exactly the right size and shape to go down into the stomach and then no further. He had three surgeries. Then there was Happy, the Edwinsons' dachshund, who ate a piece of lingerie that on removal was determined not to belong to Mrs. Edwinson. Awkward!

But the most recent entrant into the "He Ate What?!" Hall of Fame was Bouncer Rodgers. Bouncer was an aptly named young black Lab cross who was actually seen by one of my colleagues in the practice rather than by me, but I was there, and I know she won't mind me telling this story.

Bouncer was rushed in by Mrs. Rodgers one otherwise quiet Monday afternoon. "I don't know what's wrong with him! He was fine this morning, and then just now I found him staggering, barely able to stand!"

Sure enough, although Bouncer could walk, he was extremely wobbly and kept falling over. His pupils were dilated, and he had a facial expression that could only be read as pathetic confusion. As Bouncer was young and otherwise healthy, my colleague immediately suspected poisoning and told Mrs. Rodgers that the next step was to induce vomiting. Mrs. Rodgers readily agreed, and the hapless Bouncer was taken into the treatment area to have his stomach emptied.

It's not always that easy to induce vomiting (nor is it always recommended — check with a veterinarian before trying to do it yourself), but with Bouncer, it was gratifyingly easy and gratifyingly productive. Out came an enormous wad of green plant material and a small shiny tan coloured object.

Marijuana.

And a condom.

My colleague debated briefly how to present this information to Mrs. Rodgers, a conservative-looking middle-aged woman, but decided that the direct approach is always the best. There was a moment of silence as Mrs.

Rodgers processed it. After being reassured that Bouncer would quickly make a full recovery, her facial expression changed from concern to bewilderment to dawning realization to anger in a matter of seconds. It was like watching time-lapse video of weather systems.

"My son! My son's room is in the basement. Bouncer was down there this morning."

An hour or so later, a very tall, very skinny, very ashen-faced red-haired teenager came in to check on Bouncer. He didn't say anything to his mother, and he studiously avoided making eye contact with any of the staff.

## ABOUT A DUCK

His name was Puddles. His photo still hangs on the wall above my desk. Our relationship began, like so many, with a phone call from a client.

"Philipp, Mrs. Wickland is on the phone. She wants to know whether you'll see a duck."

This immediately got my attention. To be honest, I sometimes only half tune in to what I'm being told as I attempt to catch up on my office work by ineptly multi-tasking. I put down my pen and turned to face the receptionist. "Did you say duck?"

"Yup, a duck."

I picked up the phone. "Hi there, Dr. Philipp Schott speaking. I understand you have a duck now?"

"Yes! His name is Puddles! I got him from my daughter. The house was so empty after Al and Bandit died."

Al was her husband and Bandit their dog. Al had been an interesting guy and was always one of my favourite clients. He was short and round and had a gravelly voice. He was probably in his sixties, and you could tell he used to be quite muscular. He told me that he had once been a biker and that if I ever needed help dealing with a difficult client, I should ask him because he "still knew some guys" who would straighten things out. I limited my response to a smile and a nod. He also wanted to know whether he could volunteer to walk dogs for us at Christmas. We didn't have any patients stay over that Christmas, and then Al died of cancer the next year.

It turned out that there was nothing wrong with Puddles, and that Mrs. Wickland just wanted him to get a check-up. So I read up on ducks as best as I could in advance, and then on the appointed day Puddles waddled in the front door, herded gently by Mrs. Wickland. Puddles was a standard white farm duck. Have you ever been up close to one? They are surprisingly large. He was easily ten pounds, and when he stood tall he reached halfway up my thigh. Now imagine the scene in the waiting room. A half dozen clients, a couple dogs, a couple cats, and in walks a duck. You could pretty much see the pupils of the cats' eyes dilate from across the room. One dog was indifferent while the other, a little Cairn terrier, began barking furiously until the owner settled him down. Puddles was as cool as a proverbial cucumber. He ignored everyone, let out a few soft quacks, strutted (a waddling kind of strut, mind you) about the waiting room and generally assumed the air of having claimed the place.

The examination went well, despite Puddles's clear indignation at aspects of it, and I was able to pronounce him healthy, although I was at pains to make it clear to Mrs. Wickland that I was far from being a duck expert. The years went by, and Puddles came in regularly for his check-ups and once or twice for relatively minor foot and skin issues. I always looked forward to his visits. I shouldn't play favourites among my patients, but he was definitely a favourite. He was treated like a rock star by the staff and the other clients, and his arrival never failed to spark delighted gasps.

Then one day Mrs. Wickland called to say that Puddles wasn't well. He had been eating less and less, and his bowel movements were much wetter than normal. When I looked at him it was obvious that he had lost weight, and he wasn't nearly as feisty as he usually was. Also, it became clear that it wasn't watery stool she had seen, but excessive urination mixing with the stool. We ran some tests and determined that his kidneys were failing. He was eight years old at that point, which is elderly for a duck. We struggled along with a few attempts at treatment as Mrs. Wickland wasn't ready to say goodbye yet, but nothing made any difference. With tremendous sadness, one blustery March day, we let Puddles go.

Spring is a busy time, so despite his celebrity status, I soon stopped thinking about Puddles until six months later when Mrs. Wickland phoned. I hadn't spoken to her since the day of the euthanasia. She had trouble keeping the emotion out of her voice, but she wanted reassurance that she had done everything she possibly could for him. She missed him terribly, and she always would. Love is blind. It is blind to gender, colour, age, shape, religion, and it is absolutely blind to species.

# EPILOGUE

HAIKU FOR MY DOG

*Barker at the dawn;*
*Thief of snacks and foul tissues;*
*Soft brown eyes meet mine.*

We have cats whom we love dearly and who deserve to have their stories told as well, but this is about my dog — my first dog, so many years after my boyhood dreams. His name is Orbit, and it's his birthday today.

I didn't think we were ready for a dog. We were busy people with two young children and two dog-averse cats. We both worked, and we travelled a lot. But my daughter changed our minds. "When will I ever get a dog?" she sobbed. This woke something in me that had been sleeping for 40 years.

As intended, Orbit was my daughter's dog. She loved him so much. She brushed him and fed him and helped train him and walked him at least some of the time. But then, in almost imperceptible increments, this changed. Did the novelty slowly wear off for her, as everyone said it would? Did he grow on me in soft, stealthy steps, as everyone said he would? Yes, both, I think. My daughter still loves him very much, of course, but I love him now too, fiercely even. I brush him and feed him and walk him and spend a ridiculous portion of the commute home looking forward to his greeting. And the hilarious thing is that he isn't even objectively a "good dog." He's actually a bit of an idiot. But he is a lovable idiot, and, naïve as I know it might be, I manage to believe that his heart is pure. And this is really all that matters.

So now when I enter an exam room and see a dog sitting beside their human companion, I have a more personal and immediate sense of what can pass between the two of them.

Thank you for this, Orbit. And for those greetings and dawn walks and everything else. Happy birthday.

# ACKNOWLEDGEMENTS

I could go one of two ways in thanking people. I could craft an exhaustive list of family and friends and teachers and professors and bosses and mentors and colleagues and staff and clients and patients who have positively influenced my career or my writing and have thereby contributed to this book. This list would quite literally go on for pages. Nobody wants to read that. And I would inevitably forget someone.

So instead, I will go the second way and just highlight the ones who have made the largest difference.

I am the veterinarian I am today in large measure due to the mentorship of two extraordinary colleagues: Dr. Barb Deviaene and the late Dr. Bob Brandt. School teaches the science of veterinary medicine, but you need to work with people like Barb and Bob to learn the *art* of veterinary medicine.

And I am the writer I am today at least in part due to my mother. Praise was scarce in my house when I was growing up. The unspoken default expectation was that we would do well. No need to talk about it. Consequently, I was floored when one day after seeing an A+ on an essay my mother told me that she thought I had always had a knack for writing. I'm sure she doesn't even remember that stray remark, but it stuck with me and became my lodestone.

I also would like to thank my publisher, Jack David, for making what I had assumed would be an arduous process so easy and even enjoyable.

Finally, I do have to thank my clients and their pets. There is no way to pick out a few, so I will thank all of them together. With their trust and patience, they have made my career and they have made this book. These are their stories.